A Guide to Open311

A Guide to Open311

A new channel of public services for
Non-Emergency Civic Service

RAKESH PATEL

PARTRIDGE
A Penguin Random House Company

ISBN: Hardcover   978-1-4828-4636-2
               Softcover   978-1-4828-4637-9
               eBook   978-1-4828-4635-5

Print information available on the last page.

To order additional copies of this book, contact
Partridge India
000 800 10062 62
orders.india@partridgepublishing.com

www.partridgepublishing.com/india

CONTENTS

INTRODUCTION

The world today is facing a plethora of problems which can only be addressed by the inhabitants of the planet itself. Be it a developed nation with a strong institutional and structures or a third-world developing country, which is still going through the struggle of establishing itself, each faces its own unique set of troubles that can be collectively pacified by the planning and action of the responsible government and the involvement of the citizens of the country itself. This brings about the critical need for civic services. Broadly, civic services, or civics, can be defined as the rights and duties of the citizens to each other and to the country, through the medium of the elected governing body.

Most civic services, on a global scale, are emergency-related services, for example, activities targeted at disaster relief, but not to be undermined, non-emergency civic services are equally important. Non-emergency civic duties comprise of activities that are targeted at improving situations where there is no danger to life or there is no need for urgent medical attention. Examples of non-emergency civic services are crime reporting, provision of education, jury duty, voting, etc. But for civic services to be effective, one necessary condition has to be met, and that essential condition is about democracy, where the people of a nation have a say in every decision regarding their country, as civic service is fundamentally the empowerment of the people.

Once an environment ideal for a civic service has been established, the question that arises next, is how making a civic activities convenient and more efficient at achieving the targets that it aims for, and to find ways to maximize their impact. Technology is of utmost significance when aiming to increase the accessibility and efficiency of any service. In order to nurture the technology and innovation, both the public and private forms of investment in research and development are essential, specifically for civic services. This investment can be seen to be fruitful as evidenced by the existing helpful platforms and applications, for example open311.

The book begins by giving a general overview of what civics are? Thereby giving the readers a clear understanding of the subject matters. It also touches upon civic participation, emphasizing on the dire need for it, how to ensure it and what significant impacts result from it. It then goes on to discuss the emergence and impact of the global civics. Global civics refer to the concept of the reality of the 'world society' and highlights the rights and responsibilities of the citizens of this society towards each other. The existence of these certain duties is termed as a 'social contract' among all the world citizens.

The world society has emerged mainly due to the increasing interdependence and interaction among the various countries of the world, brought about by the advent of technological advancements and innovations which are erasing the boundaries between the countries. After tending to the topic of global civics, the section goes on to explore the classification of non-emergency civic services and clarifies the definition of these services. It also provides a detailed list of non-emergency situations. The discussion of non-emergency civic services are then further strengthened by outlining the different types of services, given along with it the famous examples of existing non-emergency services, and then educates the reader on how to access these services through different applications and platforms.

After the meaning and forms of civic services have been established, the next section focuses on civic engagement and the relationship between civic engagement and non-emergency services. Civic engagement is defined as active participation, involvement and promotion of civic services through educating and informing the community about its role and the tools at its disposal. Politically and non-politically, make a difference in the quality of the life in the society they are living in. Civic engagement has been proved to improve the quality of living in countries where it is widely practiced; among other things, mostly by decreasing the unemployment rate.

So, it can be determined that a civic engagement is not only beneficial socially but is also economically favorable. Civic engagement can be broken down into various forms, each as effective as the other, ranging from public scholarship and community development of advocacy and community service and volunteerism.

Civic engagement is only possible through participation in civic learning. Civic learning educates individuals about their responsibilities and abilities with respect to lending a hand in the betterment of their society and also enabling individuals to effectively understand the social, economic and political realities of the community which they are a part of. Furthermore, in order for an individual's civic learning to be complete, it is imperative that they have complete knowledge about their rights and duties with respect to the government, only when the citizens get involved in the governing process, the power of the official will be held accountable and the betterment of the community will be ensured.

This awareness of an individual's responsibility, capabilities and identification of the aspects of the community that needs improvement cannot be isolated from the effectiveness of civil services, in both the emergency and non-emergency situations, which can only be brought about when a citizen is fully informed.

To assist every form of non-emergency civic services, diverse varieties of platforms and applications have been created and are readily available. One of the emerging popular applications is a cloud based application called 'Open311'. Open311 is an advanced platform that provides users in varying parts of the world, mainly the United States of America, with open channels of communication primarily for issues related to public services. Open311 is a standardized protocol for location-based collaborative issue-tracking and serves the purpose of providing a platform where community related issues can attract attention and be reported.[1]

Open311 has a number of open channels like Service Tracker, The Daily Brief, 311 labs, etc., along with several third-party applications like Chicago Works, Fix311. Open311 is also increasingly becoming essential in relation to non-emergency civic services, establishing it as the future of such services. Apart from the existing applications of Open311, there are many others in the pipeline in the form of numerous projects related to mobile clients and server software.

Overall, this book presents the reader with a detailed understanding of what exactly civic services are, specifically non-emergency civic services. Along with informing the readers about what civic services entail and how to get involved in them, this book also brings them up-to-date with the latest and imminent innovations and platforms designed to assist civic service activities and to encourage civic engagement, today and in the future.

---

[1]   "A Collaborative Model and Open Standard for Civic Issue Tracking", Open311.

CHAPTER 1

Non Emergency Civic Service

What is Civics?

The concept of civics, or civic services, can be derived from sociological and anthropological discussions, broadly, it relates to an understanding of social science. Civic service refers to the activities carried out by the constituents of a country, aimed at the betterment of their society, along with an awareness regarding their social rights, duties and responsibilities of being a part of a constitutional democracy. Civic services can be most aptly described as the foundation of a democratic society and how it functions[2].

When the citizens of a democratic country exercise their political control, they engage in a civic service. They become involved in the government by the means of their voting rights, the right to protest and petition and through the freedom of speech. Freedom of speech is achieved primarily through the media, which is not pressured or influenced by the government in any way and is free to write the realities

---

[2]   "Civic Literacy", Pier Institute, Yale University.

of the policies that the government implements. There are no restraints on what the media says, even if it criticizing the government's actions.

Law and order also have an essential role to play in civics as they uphold and enforce justice. All these components of civics work together to ensure that the government is held accountable for all its actions and that it implements policies that are not unrepresentative of the public.

It can be derived from the above that civics essentially mean to educate the citizens of a country about their duties and responsibilities. Some examples of civic service include exercising the power to vote, fulfilling jury duty, attending town hall meetings and the form of the government and the design of the electoral system. All of the activities mentioned above are essential stepping stones of becoming involved in civics. To start with, a citizen must vote and bring to power those government officials who most accurately represent them.

In order to vote, an individual must gain complete knowledge about every candidate vying for an official position, along with being fully informed about the position and ideology for a particular candidate who stands for. This ensures that the candidate that comes to power will work for the causes that most accurately address the concerns of the citizens. After the formation of a truly public representative government, the next civic service a citizen must perform is carrying out a jury duty. Completing a jury duty ensures that the individual is part of the legal process of the country and also ensures that law and order is enforced 'by the people and for the people'.

Similarly, attending town hall meetings is another obligation that a citizen must fulfill. By attending town hall meetings, a citizen is able to provide feedback regarding important issues concerning the public and is also able to directly influence decisions regarding any new policies that the government is considering. These activities, among others, fully ensure that the citizens of a country are fully in charge of their own governance, even if the final decisions are being made by the government official.

If looked from a wider perspective, it is apparent that the practice of civics, aims to achieve a form of decentralized government in which the power does not lie in the hands of any one individual or a privileged group of individuals. So civics, if summarized, can be said to be concerned with the balance of power, along with the being the study of the obligations and rights of a citizen[3].

One important point that must be kept in mind is, often there is a misconstrued perception that civics are concerned mainly with the state and the nation. The fact that is often ignored is the importance of a city as a phase of government. A city derives its significance from the fact that it is the only phase of government with which every individual interacts, unlike the government, and it directly deals with community life. The state or government differs from

---

[3]   "Civics", Wikipedia.

the city in exactly this respect; the government is not a community, it is merely an artificial entity compared to a community[4]. So there should be no doubt as to the real target of civic services, the target being the city and the community.

Civic participating and awareness about an individual's civic responsibility is important if any democracy or philanthropy wishes to be successful. Furthermore, the citizens, by engaging in civic services, make sure the values of democracy stated in the Constitution of The United States, along with the Bill of Rights, are upheld and guaranteed. These responsibilities can be outlined as duties related to freedom, diversity, justice, equality, privacy, authority, property, truth, due process, participation, patriotism, tolerance, human rights, mutual assistance, rule of law, self-respect and finally, self-restraint. The teachings of civic responsibility in schools are encouraged, so that the educational institutes are able to produce citizens who are active and responsible participants of the government and the community.

The civic services can certainly and most strongly be related to the philanthropic sector. It is mostly nonprofit companies that benefit from the active participation and donation of citizens in the civic services. The key ideas that are related to civic participation and responsibility are service learning, civic education and volunteer work.

---

[4]   Fitzpatrik, Edward. 'What is Civic Education?'

Global Civics

With the continuous advances and breakthroughs in the technology and innovation, there has been a fast-paced increase in the interdependence of and interaction between all the countries of the world. Examples of this interconnectedness are evident all over the world. One prominent example is the effect that the well-being of the economy of America, being one of the superpowers, has on the rest of the country. A boom in the economy of America translates into a healthy economic activity in China through flourishing trade between the two countries, this leads to increased economic activity in China, resulting in increased employment opportunities and ultimately concluding in an increase in the standard of living.

The above example shows how the governance and well-being of one country affects the well-being of another country, irrespective of the boundaries and geography. This increasing sense of affinity between countries has led to the emergence of the phenomenon of a 'Global village' in which each country and community is connected and aware of one another, not only economically, but also socially and politically[5].

This emergence of a Global village brings about the necessity of global civics. Civics, which by definition is applicable to the community in which a citizen is living, need to expand to encompass the Global village, as

---

[5]   Altinay, Hakan, (2014). 'How Do We Survive and Prosper In an Interdependent World?'

the Global village, in a sense, is also a community. Global civics are a form of a social contract between the citizens of this Global village and comprises of the rights and duties that the citizens of the global community have towards each other[6].

It is important to harness this sense of global community and shared responsibility and use it to address some critical issues facing the world, issues concerning environmental and climate-related issues like global warming and climate change, along with the nuclear proliferation. Issues like the ones mentioned endanger the lives of all the inhabitants of this world and so it is imperative that they be addressed by the world as a whole. This can only be done with the growth of the global civics.

Global civics act as a form of a moral compass, a guideline of principles to present to the citizens of this interconnected world. If increasing efforts are made to follow these guiding principles, it will be easier to manage the issues that affect our planet as a whole and will put at ease the minds of its inhabitants. These guidelines, most importantly, include a set framework of rights and responsibilities of each citizen that if taken on, by the individuals, will benefit the world as a whole.

However, the idea of formation of a global framework guideline has not gone unchallenged, they must be addressed in order to gain a thorough understanding of the essence of a global civics. The first challenge that poses a threat to the concept of global civics is

---

[6]   'Global Civics', Wikipedia

a group that advocates the development of a federal world government. They believe that the issues facing our world can only be managed through the formation of a global institution. This group of people does not have faith in the workings of the nation-states and refuses to accept that a cooperation and allegiance between different nation-states are equally competent for addressing the problems of this global society.

The advocates of the world government make individuals, who otherwise trust the cooperative abilities of each nation-state, begin to question the legitimacy of those nation-states and undermine the effectiveness of the existence of an international framework followed by each individual country. The second threat to global civics is supporters of 'radical cosmopolitanism'. Radical cosmopolitanism is defined as the idea that a person should be willing to give up all of their wealth up to the point that no one person is worse-off than another person.

This ideology poses a direct threat to capitalism, which promotes that each individual gets what they earn and intimidates a rational person to avoid any conversation regarding global frameworks, a fear born out of the reality that human beings are imperfect and selfish and if they are open to the ideas of a global set of guidelines, they would have to follow the ideals of radical cosmopolitanism. Another group of people who pose a danger to the existence of global civics and the benefits that arise from the practice of civics are cynical realists. These realists promote that the world is unfair and it is foolish to try to tackle the prevailing inequity in life.

The proponents of this thought are mostly individuals who belong to the industrialist countries and have already secured a financially and socially comfortable and powerful position in the society. These individuals seek to protect the existing status quo and in turn, their own standings and oppose the concept of global civics purely out of apprehension that their own situation would change for the worse. But these groups of thought can very easily be dealt with, if more awareness is raised about the dire need of the global civics, a task which is not entirely difficult considering the innumerable threats to human life as whole.

These threats range from climate change, food, and water and fuel security to disastrous nuclear wars which would not favor any group of individuals and would affect every human being equally sooner or later.

To aid the process of determining what exactly global civics would entail, Hakan Altinay, who coined the term 'global civics', engages in two extremely insightful thought experiments. One of the thought experiments proposed by Altinay revolves around the idea of imagining how an individual would, after 1000 days, welcome the seventh-billion human being who will join this planet. The individual has to inform this new human being about the conditions of this planet that awaits them. This exercise will enable an individual to realize the present situations of this world and how they have themselves contributed to the formation of these situations.

First, the individual has to start by listing down all the good things and experiences that the newcomer should expect. This might include the advances due to technology in every aspect of life, for example, a life expectancy of above 70 years of age as compared to the lowest life expectancies of the previous eras. But in order to give a holistic view of the world, the individual will also have to inform the newcomer about the threats they will have to face in this advanced world. These threats could range from horrific genocides, grueling wars, impending food and water security issues, climate change perils that pose a danger to human life and lastly, the ever looming threat of nuclear war which could lead to the extinction of half of mankind.

This introspection will help the individual to clearly define what duties and responsibilities fall under them and in doing so, will help them understand what global civics is[7]. An understanding of what global civics is will aid the citizens of this world to collectively work towards prolonging life while tackling the threats that human beings face.

Civic Participation and Empowerment

Civic participation, i.e. when the citizens of a society actively participate in the civic services, along with the civic empowerment, it is extremely important in order to make the civic services a truly effective. What civic participation aims to achieve is instilling a sense of democratic ownership of the state processes in the

---

[7]   Altinay, Hakan, 'A Case for Global Civics".

citizens of a country. The only way to actually empower citizens and encourage civic service participation is through providing the citizens with the means of accessing and actively engaging in the public sphere.

A fully empowered society is one, in which the citizens have a full control over the political processes and they hold the government accountable to them, the media is independent of all the state influences and is empowered enough to bring about a social and a political change; every individual, whether rich or poor, is equally well-informed and thus makes an intelligent political and social decision where the law and justice is upheld and enforced.

The participating citizens of an empowered society, not only enjoy to control over the policy-making processes, that affect their wellbeing, an empowered society and its institutions are also better equipped to address any possible violent conflicts that endanger any aspect of the society. It does so by providing the public with a platform through which any conflict and argument can be resolved through dialogue and discussion instead of loss incurring clashes. If the public does not have the option of availing such a platform, there are fewer checks on disputes and violent occurrences, as instead of solving an issue through dialogue, individuals may be tempted to resolve it through violence.

In societies where there is a prevalence of the civic participation, every kind of minority groups also feel safe and no one group of individuals has an ultimate power, which they can manipulate for their own purposes, leading to a more economically and socially equal society.

There are a multitude of approaches to a civic participation and empowerment. One approach is to engage in a civil society development. A civil society is defined as a space between individuals and the government body and it enables the public, and any non-profit voluntary organizations or campaigns, to indulge in activities which empower the public in terms of informing them of their rights and reminding them of their duties. A civil society also offers a platform for a civic participation to the citizens.

Examples of such civil society organizations are charities, advocacy campaigns, community groups, faith based organization, nongovernmental organizations, etc. Most of these organizations come into being when there is a vacuum in public service delivery and the formation of such a civil society organizations becomes the only means of survival for such communities. These organizations perform the vital role of being a link between the citizens of a country and the government and they work hard to represent the social, political, cultural and ethical wants and needs of the individuals that they represent to the governing body and thereby, bringing the influence of the citizens to the governmental decision making.

Not only do they act as a bridge between the state and its people, they also perform the important task of educating and mobilizing the citizens of a society for civic participation, through which the public can then bring about a social reform pertaining to an important issue, be it economic or environmental, and reconcile any conflicts. Active civic participation, then ensures the collective welfare of all the constituents of a democracy, performing the central role of a public service delivery and helps in making the society more harmonious and economically prosperous.

However, civil society organizations on their own cannot ensure citizen empowerment and effective participation. Such organizations need to be backed by complementing and protective legal structures which, while safeguarding the organization from exploitation, also enhance their abilities and impact, making them more efficient. Such legal structures make these legitimate organizations and makes them more trustworthy for the public, safeguarding them from the public mistrust. Fundamentally, a legal framework concerning civic participation and empowerment should include laws to protect the rights of the civic participants, mainly the right to freedom of expression, information and association.

Another important aspect of the civic participation is that it should be fully inclusive. Cities and societies are made up of a diverse range of cultures, nationalities, races and ethics. So a mix of civil society organizations should exist, which do not exclude any possible faction of people, in order to fully represent the diverse population of every society. It is especially important for these organizations to concentrate more on the rights and duties of a marginalized groups and communities, for example women, a minority religious group, etc.

Such comprehensive representations of the society help bridge the gaps between people of different backgrounds and also aid in ensuring the making of a more harmonious society, which is better equipped to tackle issues of greater importance, issues concerning the overall economy or security of a country. It is important for a civil society organizations, if they originate from the international community, to focus on the community-specific needs. Such programs, then foster the growth of a leadership in the domestic community itself. They encourage and empower every individual for effective civic participation.

Lastly, even though civil society organizations are perceived as organizations that work for the collective good of the society, there is a need for corporate governance mechanisms to keep them in check as well. Examples of such a mechanism are audits or the formation of a board of directors that overlooks the operations of the organization. This ensures that even these organizations do not have an ulterior motive of their own.

Similar guidelines and rules should be applied to other institutions and organizations that enable civic participation, like the media and the formation of political parties, making sure that they are accountable, inclusively representative of all communities within the society and most importantly, ensuring that they are effective[8].

---

[8]   'Civic Participation and Empowerment', United States Institute of Peace.

It is only when there is a sense of empathy and a need to address the prevailing ills of a society in the public that they are willing to struggle to become empowered and participate in the civic activities. Without such a sense of responsibility, important decisions about who deserves and gets what resource are left to the people who work only for their own benefit and who ensure only the betterment of a select few. Such a society will eventually dissolve into chaos and will pave the way for the disastrous results of widespread poverty and anguish.

Non-emergency Situations

What can be classified as a non-emergency situation?

In order to understand what classifies as a non-emergency situation, we need to distinguish it from an emergency situation. An emergency situation, in simple terms, can be defined as any situation that poses an immediate threat to life and property. Hence, when there is no immediate threat to life, property or environment, the situation will be a non-emergency situation. There are two key terms here, which are threat and immediate. If your life or property is not facing a direct threat, then there is no emergency, similarly if you do not need an immediate response from the police or the hospital and can handle the situation on your own, this is a non-emergency.

Let us look at some real life non-emergency scenarios that will give us a better understanding of what constitutes as a non-emergency situation.

Mr. Banks returns from a week long Christmas break. As he pulls into his driveway, he notices that the front window of his house is broken and the light of the reception is turned on. As he walks into his house, he calls on the possible intruders, however, receives no reply and does not hear any noise that would indicate the presence of intruders in the premises. He inspects the whole house and finds all his belongings in place, except for the kitchen where the refrigerator is missing a few food items. Mr. Banks picks up his phone to call the emergency service. So now, the question arises whether or not the circumstances that Mr. Banks faces can be accounted as an emergency situation.

Let us review the key factors. Mr. Banks do not face a threat to his life or property anymore. In addition, the trespassers have fled the scene of the crime and there are no suspects, hence, the situation is a non-emergency situation. On the other hand, if the suspect was still on scene, Mr. Banks had every right to call the emergency services.

Calvin headed back from the academic block of the university to the parking area, as he was about to get into the car, he noticed that the car had been hit by another vehicle from the back which had left a deep dent on the left rear end of the car. Calvin noticed that other cars in the lot were parked far away from his own and In addition, were in perfect shape indicating that none of them could have been a part of this hit and run incident. As there is again no danger to Calvin's life, no prevailing threat to his property and the fact that the suspected driver is not present at the scene anymore, the situation will be classified as a non-emergency. It is preferable for Calvin to register a complaint on the non-emergency line of the police, instead of reaching out the emergency services.

A person or a thing that is causing inconvenience or is a source of annoyance is termed as a nuiSansce. Most acts of nuiSansce fall under non-emergency situations such as those mentioned in the following scenarios. At such instances, immediate assistance of the police is not required and a complaint concerning the nuiSansce can be registered later. Also these situations are not red alerts as they do not pose a threat to a person's life or property.

Ms. Catherine wakes up in the middle of the night because of the loud music her neighbors are playing, she steps out of her house to view the situation and finds that the young couple living next door are hosting their anniversary party and over 30 cars are parked in the street. Ms. Catherine is infuriated when she sees two of the cars parked in her driveway and some paper cups and other trash that has been thrown in her garden. She decides to reach the emergency services to call the police, however the situation at hand does not pose a threat to her life and although there have been some property breaches, nothing has been damaged, so it is a non-emergency situation that can be taken care of by registering a complaint the next morning.

Mr. Xavier shuts down his grocery store and proceeds towards his car; his car is parked at the backside of the store. While getting into his car, Mr. Xavier notices graffiti on the back wall of his store. He gets off to inspect it and sees that the spray paint has dried off and there is no lingering smell of the paint. He looks around and sees no one within a distant mile so he decides to contact the police in the morning and registers a complaint. Mr. Xavier has made the right decision. Although part of his property has been damaged, there lies no other threat and the felons have left the premises so there are no possible suspects. Hence, the situation is a non-emergency one.

Ms. Franklin misplaced her credit card and has no idea how long the card has been missing or where it is likely to have gone missing. In addition, she usually gets a notification via email each time the card is swiped and has received no such notification. As there is reasonable doubt that the card may still be in her possession and also does not pose a serious threat to Miss Franklin, it is advisable that she avoids alerting the emergency services and rather calls the respective financial institution and blocks the card.

Numerous other situations such as family fights or feuds, minors violating curfews, missing adults, underage drinking, reports of vandalism and drug abuse by teenagers are all examples of a non-emergency situations. In certain scenarios, the designated staff of the organization can also tackle the situations at hand, for instance, Calvin could have reported the incident to the university's security officials who could have obtained footage from the cameras and would have assessed the whole scene.

Non-emergency civic services

So now we have to determine that what could act as an alternative to seek an emergency service of the police and the paramedics. The most notable solution is to tackle these non-emergency situations as a group by seeking the assistance of the community we abide in. This would not only ensure the participation of every member of the society to contribute positively, but is also the most efficient way to address non-emergency situations.

A system on the lines of emergency service provider, such as the 911 can be built to engage the civic services of the people of a particular town or city. First a striking helpline number such as 1212 or 2010 needs to be setup so that all the phone calls and messages can be directed to this helpline. In this day and age, a web link is mandatory so, people can get a chance to register as a member of the service and also get to know more about what the function of this provision is. An example of a non-emergency service provider is Open311, which is present in over 20 cities worldwide.

This system will allow anybody in the community to report a problem. Other members would be encouraged to add more information to the database concerning the problems, for instance a broken tree that is blocking the town highway, now anybody can report this problem and an alert would be sent out to all of the service and provider members and in this manner, anyone in his/her own capacity will remove the tree from the freeway or the authority responsible for the task, such as the traffic department, could undertake the task and hence, a non-emergency situation which could pose a possible threat to people of the community is resolved smoothly.

Let us explore some real life instances, which can be classified as non-emergency situations that were overcome by engaging civic services of the people.

Tom reported on the Rescue 1212 helpline that a dead ibex is blocking the left lane of the 4th highway. He stated that he spotted the ibex blocking the road while he was taking his daughter to the hospital and added that it posed a threat to the drivers as it was blocking the road just after a sharp turn. The service sent an alert to all of its community members and Tim, an employee of the forest department, was notified. The barrier was removed from the few hours of the report.

After a local football match, some of the angry fans trashed the local street park by uprooting the benches, throwing trash in the fountain and damaging the swings. Andy took pictures of the vandalized area and registered a report to Savethecity (local non-emergency service provider) through the STC mobile application. All members of the community who had signed up on STC were forwarded the pictures and Mr. Smith, representative of a park and recreation department of the city council, sent a green signal ensuring the restoration of the park at the earliest.

The school bus driver of the green field high, asked for assistance after the bus broke down on the way to the school, through the better ponsiville service. Within minutes, several locals who received the report reached to transport the children to school and a call was made to the school, which sent the maintenance staff over to the location.

The better ponsiville service also launched a campaign called white out, engaging its members and the local community to report graffiti on town walls and street sides and encouraged people to wash-down the graffiti by painting over it.

Another such problem was registered with a non-emergency service provider. When a stop sign had been uprooted by a storm the night before at a main intersection, a message was sent out to all affiliates. A lady living in a nearby plot replied that the stop sign was lying in her yard after which the emergency service provider registered a complaint with the traffic department giving them all the necessary information after the stop sign was reinstalled.

Not only are these service providers giving community members an opportunity to be involved, but this also guarantees the accountability of the local administration and municipal authority.

If a reported problem is not taken care of within a set time, a complaint against the authorities can be registered and in addition, the higher ups could also be made aware of the fact that their workers or employees are not working efficiently. This would also reduce the increased workload on emergency service providers such as 911 and will help them reorganize and improve their work.

In the section concerning non-emergency situations, we discussed that nuiSansces are usually categorized under non-emergency situations. A great way to tackle such instances is through the complaint service of the non-emergency providers.

If we look at the situation concerning the loud party thrown by a particular neighbor, instead of approaching the police, a complaint could be registered with the local service provider, which could consult other neighbors about the extent of the problem and after taking confirmation from others, send a notification to the certain party to be careful in the future. Security and safety situations that don't pose a direct threat to life, property or the environment can be resolved by employing non-regency civic services.

In some model cities and towns, responsibility is taken by neighbors alternately to keep a check on the others property, especially when the specific resident is away on holidays or business trips. Here, the community will act as the security alarm system and ensure that the person's property is kept safe and secure.

In conclusion, non-emergency situation can be easily overcome by the power of the local community. In addition, it inspires and encourages the citizens to become more involved and a true sense of community, where each person is contributing as well as benefitting from the actions of his neighbors, is formed. However, it is important to spread awareness about such service providers so that a maximum number of community members can become a part of such operations.

How to Summon a Non-Emergency Service

There are multiple ways and techniques of availing the facilities of a non-emergency service. Most non-emergency services usually extensively advertise themselves on television or newspapers in order to make themselves accessible to the public. In these advertisements, they provide all the contact details necessary to summon a non-emergency service when required. One well-known example is that of a police hotline where people can report the occurrences of any crimes they witness.

For example, suppose a family comes home from a week's vacation, only to find that they have been robbed. They would immediately contact their respective area's police department and report the burglary. It would then be the responsibility of the police force to carry out an investigation and bring to justice the culprits of the crime. Once the police are successful in capturing the robbers, the family will feel more secure. Similarly, numerous other hotlines have been set up all around the world to address issues of various natures, be it reporting a crime or a phone line set up to address and calm down suicidal citizens.

Another method of summoning non-emergency civic services are through utilizing the digital platforms.

There are various websites and SNS pages that act as forums for contacting non-emergency services. Digital platforms are also more convenient than the traditional method of calling non-emergency services because of an online platform, users can access a flush of information and easily pinpoint the non-emergency service that is most suited to them. Another function of the internet and digital platforms is that they simultaneously act as databases of information and are more efficient means of raising civic awareness.

An example of such a platform for civic services is the numerous forums that the organization of the United Nations (UN) has. In these forums, individuals from diverse backgrounds can educate themselves about the prevailing issues in their society, and the world that can also engage in dialogues with other people from around the world. Such constructive conversations result in improved understanding between different communities. There are also many other forums which act as a bridge between the government and the citizens. Through these platforms, the citizens may voice their grievances to the government and raise awareness about the public concerns.

There are several drawbacks to the conventional methods of accessing non-emergency services. As the most popular method is through a phone call, most individuals will find that they may not be able to get through to the service they are trying to call. This could result in a decrease in the efficiency and impact of the non-emergency services. Similarly, the forums and platforms provided by the internet may not be entirely effective, as most of the time, the authenticity of the civic service related affairs is questionable.

But there are several applications being developed that can be used to summon a non-emergency service and can be conveniently accessed through either cell phones or the internet. One such application is Open311. Open311 is an advanced form of technology that provides various open channels of communication where issues regarding public space and public services can be reported. Open311 is a step above the more conventional one-to-one call-center services, in the sense that the technology for this application uses the internet and enables many-to-many interactions between services and clients. Open311 guarantees that the voices of the users are heard and encourages people from various backgrounds to openly and simultaneously trade information, regarding a specific public concern.

But that isn't the only thing that this platform does. Open311 makes sure that the technology is easily accessible to everyone and at any location where it is operating. The most developed function of Open311, at the moment, is to gather information about non-emergency issues in the public sphere. It does so by reporting and tracking any reported concern. Examples of problems that are frequently reported are problems with infrastructures like broken street lights, roads that need repair and other issues regarding pollution.

The way of using Open311 is that, any individual can spot a public concern and then report it to this platform by using their mobile device or computer to upload information that is possibly complemented with a photograph. A report is generated regarding that particular issue and is sent to the relevant authority, so that they may deal with the problem. Open311 is a marked improvement from the traditional phone line because all the information on this application is open for access by the general public. This measure makes the workings of Open311 more transparent and ensures that the authorities responsible for dealing with the reported issues are held accountable.

So overall, Open311 ensures an effective non-emergency response to civic issues and in turn, encourages people to participate and fulfill their duties of civic services. The Open311 application is currently available on the Web, Android phones, iPhones, Windows phones and Blackberry phones. As Open 311 is a new application, there is still ongoing work being done on improving the facilities offered by this application along with increasing the outreach of this service.

Currently, Open311 has many variations of its applications available in different cities of North America, namely Sans Francisco and Chicago, but its developers are actively working on making Open311 applications available on a wider scale. But, as with any new piece of technology, such innovations and improvement will take time.

CHAPTER 2

Civic Engagement

What is Civic Engagement?

Once an individual considers and identifies him bound to a social contract with the rest of his society and community, they become morally and civically aware of their possible contribution to the plethora of social problems and as a part of a social fabric, it is that individual's responsibility to engage in civic activity. This realization of civic responsibility is an essential prerequisite for a civic engagement[9]. So if defined, civic engagement is participating in activities that aim to target a social problem and improve the quality of life of a society in general.

However, civic engagement has many aspects of itself, describing diverse philosophies of citizenship and the different types of activities that come under it. The meaning of civic engagement changes for every individual, molding itself to the life experiences and social upbringing, ultimately depending upon the perspective of the person who is attempting to define

---

[9]   'The Definition of Civic Engagement', The New York Times.

it. When considered in a limited scope, there are raft definitions of civic engagement. One perspective views, civic engagement as a form of community service, characterized by a person's participation in voluntary services, whether individually or through the platform of an organization.

An example of civic engagement as a community service is when an individual donates money to an orphanage or just gives money to a homeless or needy person. A second definition of civic engagement is civic engagement through collective action. This is a very restrictive definition as it only considers civic engagement as an activity in which individuals join together to fulfill their roles and responsibilities of being a citizen and ultimately resulting in an impact on the civil society.

Another view of civic engagement is that it is a form of political engagement. This is another circumscribed view of civic engagement, limiting it to activity that not only comes about through a collaboration of citizens, but is also strictly political in nature or in other words, includes activities that involve action through the government. This view believes that social issues can be efficiently solved only through the channel of the political process.

Advocates of this view further go on to make a distinction between an individual's work to meet other people's need as a service activity and collective and public work aimed at solving social issues as civic activities and deems public leadership activities as an essential component of civic engagement, making the role of a government indispensable.

Lastly, civic engagement has been viewed as a means of social change as well. This specific definition has been aptly described by the founder of Social Capital Inc., David Crowley as: "Civic engagement describes how an active citizen participates in the life of the community in order to help shape its future. Ultimately, civic engagement has to include the dimensions of social change."[10]

Moving ahead from the limiting definitions of civic engagement, there are also extremely broad classifications of civic engagement that can be used to understand it. One view is that an amalgamation of all the narrower perspectives laid out above, is that a civic engagement is an individual or collaborative activity aimed at addressing issues and problems of social concern. Civic engagement can utilize the electoral platform and work through the established institution of a democracy, the resources of an organization or it can even be an individual effort.

Examples of a civic engagement under this definition are fulfilling your duty to vote, volunteering at a non-governmental agency that aims at correcting a specific public concern, like poverty, or by individually giving money or resources to a poor and underprivileged person. An even broader definition, proposed by Robert Putnam, expands civic engagement to include

---

[10]   Adler, P. Richard (2005), 'What Do We Mean By "Civic Engagement"?', Journal of Transformative Education.

formal and informal social activities, ranging from social calls on friends to community service and political participation. Putnam basically defines civic engagement as any form of social interaction aimed towards improving the cohesiveness of a society[11].

In an interesting study, Keeter et al. (2002) carried out an insightful investigation into the question of which generation was the most civically active. The study compared the civic engagement activities of different generations, the first one lying in the age group of 15 years to 25 years, the second one lying in the age bracket of 38 years to 55 years and the third age bracket of 55 years and above. The results of the study showed that more than 50% of the 55 years and above population was engaged in a civic activity, followed by the age group of 38 years to 55 years.

The most civically disengaged members belonged to the age group of 15 years to 25 years. But the younger generation was found to be more involved in the community service related to civic activities as compared to the electoral involvement, for example voting, of the older age groups[12].

The alarming disinterest of the younger population in civic services gives rise to the question of how

---

[11]   Putnam, R. (2000), 'Bowling Alone: The Collapse and Revival of American Community', New York: Simon & Schuster.

[12]   Keeter, S., Zukin, C., Andolina, M., & Jenkins, M. (2002). 'The Civic and Political Health of the Nation: A Generational Portrait.'

to get the younger population more involved in a civic services. For the youth enrolled in schools and colleges, it is not an extremely difficult task to get them more engaged in a civic activity. This is because most educational institutes incorporate aspects of civic learning and engagement in their curriculums, and a majority of universities consider the community service activities while evaluating their applicants for admissions.

But in many countries, there is a large portion of the youth that is not enrolled in such educational institutes. It has been advised that in order to engage the above mentioned youth, it would be fruitful to hold seminars and informative and motivating sessions at their workplaces, faith-based organizations, clubs, and etc.[13].

Forms of Civic Engagement

Any activity that can be classified as a social service with the aim of addressing a public issue or concern or attempting to educate the people as to what their rights and duties are, with regards to the society they inhibit, is a form of civic engagement. Some of the most prominent forms of community engagement are public scholarship, community development, advocacy and community service or volunteerism.

---

[13]　Flanagan, C., Levine, P., & Settersten, R.'Civic Engagement and the Changing Transition to Adulthood'.

Public scholarship refers to any sort of research that aims to improve societal living standards or serves the social interest beneficially. It is most widely practiced by university students as a part of their educational curriculum and serves the dual purpose of developing civic habits as well as advancing educational careers. Engagement in public scholarship has a set of core dimensions that outlines what exactly it aims to achieve. These core objectives are a development of a democracy, provision of the public goods, social responsibility, ownership of education and diversity[14].

The establishment of a democratic system is an essential condition for the existence of a civic service activities and it is postulated by many educated philosophers that an educated society is a cardinal precondition for an effective democracy. Through the means of a public scholarship, the population of a democratic entity will be educated and intellectually and more capable of addressing controversial public issues through dialogue and cooperation. Such an educated society can only be created through indulgence in public scholarship.

Community development can be defined as the efforts of a society itself to explore, identify and develop their economic, and most importantly, human resources through acts of, ranging from but not limited to, fundraising and charity, infrastructure development, etc. Community development helps the society as a whole to address any issues regarding financial capital,

---

[14]   Wray, D., Laura et al. (2006). 'An Explication of Public Scholarship Objectives'.

labor, infrastructure, human resource development, natural resources and creating knowledge awareness.

Overall, the community development can be thought of as a holistic approach to addressing the multiple needs of the community, i.e. improvement in the economic, social and environmental requirements of a society. But for a community development to be truly effective, the people must be united and must believe that together with the governmental authorities, they have the capability to contribute to national progress.

However, community development is not just an activity, it is a whole process, a systematic procession of activities which result in the achievement of a common goal and so it takes time and commitment and has to have guidelines and principles that ensure its effectiveness. Furthermore, community development must also be a sustainable and long term.

Advocacy is another extremely powerful form of a civic engagement. Advocacy, in general terms, involves mobilizing the general public to influence a public policy making through a formal political channel. Examples of advocacy are protests for a cause or exercising an individual's right to vote. Engaging in an advocacy, regarding whatever cause, makes the general public and their concerns more noticeable to the governing body and demands that attention be paid to the issue at hand. One of the most important tools of an advocacy that has emerged is the nonprofit organizations that work for specific causes.

Throughout the history, these nonprofit organizations have been profoundly effective in mobilizing the general public and providing them with a structured platform that conveys the message of their voices to the government and the public by the means of an efficient public relation techniques and expert research. Nonprofit advocacy organizations can also be further divided into categories of organizations that carry out issue research, organizations that work on a grass-root mobilization and lastly, organizations that engage in direct legislative lobbying. Examples of advocacy causes supported by nonprofit organizations are public education, community organization, voter education and issue and policy advocacy.

An individual can also indulge in civic engagement through the community service and volunteerism. The effects of these two civic activities are much more immediate and instant as compared to the other forms discussed. Community service and volunteer activities work on addressing and providing relief regarding the immediate concerns of the society. Not only do volunteer activities benefit the community, they also benefit the volunteers themselves.

Survey conducted by the National Survey of Giving, Volunteering and Participating (NSGVP) found that 79 percent of the volunteers found a marked improvement in their interpersonal skills, enabling them to effectively understand and motivate other people. It also helped the volunteers to prepare for dealing with the difficult social situations. Other than that, 68 percent of the volunteers also reported a vast improvement in their communication skills along with more awareness and knowledge about the issues they are volunteering for.

Volunteering has also significant employment and education related value, as community service experience is an impressive addition to an individual's resume and makes them a more preferable candidate[15]. But the facts above do not undermine the altruistic motives behind individuals who undertake volunteer work. According to a survey, only five percent students listed their reasons for volunteering as fulfilling a school requirement, the rest of the 95 percent engaged in a community service and volunteer work solely out of interest in making a difference in their community[16].

Civic engagement is not restricted to voting, attending town hall meetings and volunteer work, it also encompasses activities like educating oneself about the public policy making procedures by following the news or reading informative magazines. Even socializing with your neighbors and every other form of social connectedness is considered as a civic engagement. Furthermore, the advent of technology and the digital age has given birth to a new form of civic engagement.

The internet and social media are fast becoming another vital platform of civic participation, providing the public with an unfathomable library of information through which they can educate and constantly

---

[15]   'The Benefits of Volunteering',(2000). NSGVP
[16]   Corporation for National and Community Service, 2005.

update themselves with the current events of not just their own country, but of the world.

The emergence of another digital phenomenon, social networking sites (SNS) like Facebook and twitter, are also important developments in the form of a civic engagement. Social networking sites can be used as forums for advocacy campaigns and as a means of disseminating any form of information and knowledge to a vast majority of people all around the world. The immense popularity of these social networking sites also makes them exceedingly successful as a means of a civic engagement. Online platform also makes a simple civic engagement activities, like donating money for a cause, exceedingly simple.

Just by providing some information and a click of a button, a person in any corner of the world can easily play their part in a cause and fulfill their civic responsibility. One drawback of a civic engagement on a digital platform is that most online facilities are only accessible to the privileged or those who can afford it and so it excludes a major portion of a community's population. This somewhat lessens the impact and effectiveness of the internet and its role in civic engagement.

Similarly, beyond the digital platform, there still exists a vast majority of citizens who are isolated from the efforts of a civic engagement and so they feel powerless in the cause of working towards a common good. This calls for the need of a civic renewal movement across maximum sectors and populations. Civic renewal involves completely revamping civic engagement practices and making them more citizen-centered and moving them away from just being a set of tactics.

Instead, this revamped civic engagement would concentrate on empowering the citizens and generating opportunities through which the public comes together and works on issues of utmost importance. Every possible form of civic engagement is extremely crucial due to the continually deteriorating conditions of our world. In a world where there are continuous threats of mass genocides, loss of human lives due to famines and droughts and dangers of nuclear war to the human species, it is imperative that every means of encouraging unity is used. This unity among the human species can then be used to collectively tackle and mitigate any possible threat for as long as possible.

How Does Civic Engagement Relate to Non-Emergency Civic Services

As can be seen in the previous sections, civic engagement primarily revolves around the empowerment and active participation of citizens in activities that improve the well-being and functioning of their society. Since it is mostly civilians who engage in civic services, the nature of these services is limited to non-emergency facilities. This is apparent because situations and issues that require emergency and immediate attention are ones that require some form of technical expertise, be it doctors or trained army personnel.

So it would be safe to assume that citizens who engage in civic services do not necessarily need to have the capabilities of responding to an emergency situation. For clarification purposes, it is outlined that emergency services are those services which respond to life-threatening instances, for example a fire or relief services in response to a flood or an earthquake. Non-emergency civic services can be classified as services which address issues in which there is no immediate danger to any individual's life. Another aspect of non-emergency civic services is that the impact of the service may not be immediate and it might take some time for the effects of the non-emergency services to become apparent.

So it is apparent from the classifications given above that the citizens who want to engage in non-emergency services can be of any background and need not possess any technical degree or training. This empowers each and every constituent of a society and makes it their duty and responsibility to provide every possible kind of non-emergency services that is required of them. An example of how a citizen can engage in a non-emergency civic service can be taken for the formation of a hypothetical situation. Suppose the house next to yours is hosting a party.

As the time approaches midnight, the party at your neighbors is still in full swing and it is creating a public nuiSansce due to the amount of noise that the party is generating. You decide to take things into your own hands and call the police and report your neighbors as disturbing the neighborhood's peace. The police department responds immediately and arrives at your neighbor's house and instructs them to end the festivities. This returns the peaceful atmosphere back to the neighborhood. In this small way, you as a citizen have engaged in a civic service by undertaking a definite action and utilizing a non-emergency civic service to address an issue concerning the welfare of your community.

It can be concluded that non-emergency civic services and civic engagement are two activities that facilitate each other. Without the presence of either a citizen participating in a civic service or the non-emergency service that caters to such issues, any civic activity would have a minimal and, in some cases, negligible impact.

CHAPTER 3

Civic Learning

What is Civic Learning

Civic learning comprises of educating the members of a certain community through active participation to make decisions, draft policies, and bring reforms in the public sector. It equips the community members with the skills that will firstly enable them to identify the problems that the community faces and also the skills to draft solutions to resolve the problem. Civic learning falls under the category of service learning, which is a form of community service. The learning basically focuses on learning through field study and practical work.

A term closely linked with the civic learning is democracy or democratic ways because democracy is by the people, for the people and of the people; civic engagement, as previously discussed, talks about involving the community and letting them take decisions or make efforts that will positively affect their community.

The learning or the study aims to develop the civic character of the student and instill in them all the values that enable them to contribute positively towards their community. Civic learning aims at building an individual's civic capacity and attributes included in civic capacity are:

a) Skills such as debating, writing, listening, deliberating
b) Values such as commitment, dedication
c) Beliefs such as that, as a citizen of a said community it is our duty to serve others
d) Attitudes such as tolerance and acceptance of others
e) Disposition that is willingness to work with others

Civic learning has most of its focus on skill building in students. Skills that are developed or polished as part of a civic learning program include debating, discussing and discoursing so the student has the ability to get his viewpoint across to the audience clearly and without any ambiguity. Part of debating an issue at hand includes giving the chance to the other party to speak and hearing them out, so the listening skill of students is working on too. The students are also taught how to deliberate, that is writing down the pros and cons, weighing the reasons and cutting down options to reach one unanimous solution.

Public speaking skills are polished by letting the students who are a part of the program speak in public forums where special emphasis is laid on confidence, accuracy and clarity. The learning programs also focus on enabling the students to look at a problem from various perspectives such as social and political.

The skill of separating facts and information from speculation and conjecture is something of great importance in today's century and is worked on as a part of the civic learning program.

Civic values include all those values that help bring good to the society in some form or manner. One of the foremost civic values imparted through civic learning programs is that we all bear a collective responsibility towards one another; when we develop this sense of possibility only then are we able to identify, evaluate and deliberate on collective problems.

Since, as mentioned above, civic learning has encouraged democratic ways, a lot of focus is placed on solving issues by involving every member of the community and while doing so, treating each member with equality. If during the course of solving an issue democratically a conflict arises, it should be resolved by reaching a consensus. The discussion should have a clear direction and should lead to a solution agreed upon by the majority of people.

Civic beliefs include accepting the fact that politics is parallel to social life and cannot be excluded or eliminated, as it sprouts from the theory that at the end of the day, political discourse and involvement is the only thing that will solve problems that we face in our social life. Civic learning also trains us to be open to others' beliefs and ideas that tells us that it is the only way to reach a conclusion in the discussion or discourse.

Civic learning teaches us to mold our attitudes. Attitude is primarily a mental state that comes from our values, beliefs and experiences, and either inclines us to have a favorable or unfavorable reaction to a situation. Civic learning emphasizes that students have a positive attitude and embrace things positively; it encourages us to have a positive attitude towards others, such as mutual respect and empathy. It not only explains that we should have a positive attitude towards people, but also towards a dialogue.

Civic learning discourages arrogance or inflexibility; rather it states that there is no loss or harm in reaching a compromise, as it is everyone's victory. Civic attitude revolves around learning from others and showing flexibility, however, it also teaches us that when it is hard to reach a compromise or deliberate, it is better to accept each other's differences.

Disposition is all about achieving internal selflessness and this concept is also emphasized upon in civic learning. A person needs to place the people or community's good above the good of his or her own self. It is human nature that when we don't see a matter concerning or more importantly benefiting our lone self, we tend to ignore it, and however civic learning instills in us the spirit to participate actively in collective problem solving. It also teaches us to include others in our discussion or decision making with open arms rather than alienating them. It nurtures the spirit of working in harmony and cooperation with others and negates the concept of competitiveness.

Civic learning motivates us to approach a discussion as well as the participants in the discussion with an open mind and it signifies the importance of communicating with others rather than trying to obtain victory.

A civic learner would therefore tackle or resolve a problem much differently from a student who has not undergone service learning. Firstly, he would consider a problem faced by the community as his problem; as mentioned above he is trained to see a community as one collective body and their troubles as one collective problem; moreover, he is trained to put the problems or issues of the community over their own personal problems. He would also show willingness and an eagerness to participate actively in the dialogue.

In addition a service learner would debate with an open mind and be willing to listen and give space to the ideas of another, but at the same time will also deliver his/her ideas very effectively. If needed he/she would be ready to reach a compromise rather than arguing just for the sake of arguing. The ultimate goal that a student who has taken up civic learning would want to achieve would be to lead the discourse towards a possible solution. He would show the values of commitment and dedication to reach a goal, which have been inculcated in him through civic learning, and will deliberate by weighing reasons and finally reaching a solution that is agreed upon by a majority of the people and is welcomed positively.

Importance of Civic learning

Civic learning, as mentioned repeatedly, involves practical work. It is about experiencing a real-world challenge, taking it on and striving to tackle the situation; hence, it equips a student with the skill set needed to sort out the problems of the public and community. The experience provided to you by the practical work in the civil learning training is the only thing that will work to one's advantage rather than knowledge obtained from books or scholarly work. In short, civic learning is the only method to train an individual to take on public trials.

An important aspect of civic learning is its ability to enable students to gain life skills by exposing the students to real life situations. It also inculcates a sense of responsibility in the students about their society, community and people.

Community service, which is an integral form of civic learning, has shown positive effects on students' academic performance. Research studies have indicated that students who completed community service hours have acquired better GPAs and grades in the university, so the common belief that students lose sight of their studies due to increased community participation is invalid, as those students have turned out to perform even better in their academics.

The students revealed that the community service helped them to retain the academic material better, as they had experienced every situation first hand. Faculty and university professors also believe that this type of service learning aids students to perform better in schools and colleges; they also revealed that service learners and participants engage with more efficacy in class discussions and debate, as they link every concept or theory to their experience.

Civic learning has also shown to enhance the writing and critical thinking skills of the student as they are required to make decisions that affect a large number of people. A research study by the American Association of Community Colleges supported the argument that the service learning enhanced the academic performance. The AACC launched Horizon grantee colleges were spread across the states and the group launched a survey to compare courses that offered service learning with those that did not. The survey showed that students who were survey learners not only had a higher GPA but also took up more courses in various fields of studies.

Civic learning has also managed to motivate and inspire students to pursue a career in the service field. When the students get hands on experience of working in the real world and providing his/her services, which happens to affect the community at large, they realize that each and every step they take can make a great difference in the society they live in. Hence, it excites them to obtain a career in the service field, for instance, working in the development sector or public policy division. This is also great, as people who are trained and have experience and at the same time are extremely motivated to work for the betterment of their community, join the service field.

Students who have participated in the practical aspect of civic learning tend to convince other people to spend some of their time in community service, so more and more people are drawn towards it.

This field of study is also very significant as it helps students realize that their efforts are making an actual difference: a study in this regard showed that almost 90% of the students felt that their practical work through this field of study is actually making a difference in their community. When students actually start that their hard work or efforts could make a difference, they link it positively to their future endeavors.

Usefulness of any type of education is assessed primarily by how students will apply the knowledge they have gained when they begin their practical life. With civic learning, this opportunity is being provided to the students in their college years, so that students learn how to apply the knowledge that they have gained from books to real world circumstances, which polishes their application skills. This also diminishes the conventional method of education, which is often discouraged; memorizing from books and writing it all back down on a piece of paper during the examination. An instructor at a community college is reported to have said, "We can give them all the book knowledge they want, but if they can't use it when they leave here, what have we given them?"

A major issue that we face at workplaces is the biases or the strong beliefs that people come to, which they are not willing to change, making them incapable of accepting others. Some of these biases are rooted in an individual's background and they might have an opinion without having any arguments or information to back it, so a civic learning enables the students to get rid of their biases by replacing them with the factual information.

There has always been stress on the fact that more than anything, education is about polishing individuals to make them become better human beings, to inculcate in them humanism and empathy for other people and developing values like compassion, kindness and benevolence in them. The teachers are of the belief that this can be achieved in a better manner through engaging students in the community service. We see in our legal system the juvenile delinquents are given the community service hours as a penalty for their offences; what we need to realize is that maybe if we had exposed them to a civic learning they would have developed the civic virtues and the model, civic character that we have talked about earlier, which would eventually lead them not to commit the offense in the first place.

Teachers and professors also felt that they have been able to achieve an improved classroom environment through civic learning and training. Firstly, even the students who would not participate fully in the class discussions before do so now as every individual has had a different experience that they are eager to share. In addition, learning has become a two way process, as the teachers also get to learn from the experiences of the students. With the monotony removed, that is the teachers teaching the same course work for decades, the teachers become more zealous and all of this lets them to have a better relationship with their students.

Service learners have been noted to be great at the interviews, as all of the experience, they have gained through practical work enables them to answer questions intelligently. In addition, civic learning encompasses the polishing of public speaking skills that boosts their confidence and these candidates are able to maintain composure during the interview. Organizations therefore prefer students who have undergone civic learning, as they find those students to be more motivated, hence producing a better result in the work place and contributing positively to the atmosphere of the workplace.

The greatest and the most significant impact of the civic learning would be to retain the students in the college and motivate them to graduate with a degree. Most college goers in today's age usually end up dropping out and aborting their studies because of many factors that are distracting the student. However, when a student learns that his efforts are making a real difference to the community, it keeps him/her motivated to continue his study. Self-satisfaction and also satisfaction with their college and field of study, motivates the students to finish their studies.

Civic learning is of extreme importance, as it further enhances our education system and help students to develop skills like deliberating, whilst it also improves and polishes other skills such as writing and listening. In addition, as pointed out by teachers and instructors, it creates a great learning environment in the classrooms, as students get to relate their course to work as per their experiences, which generates a healthy discussion. It help students to become mature and responsible citizens who want to strive to work for the betterment of their community. Retention of students is also an important aspect that is an advantage of the civic learning; students who are unsure about continuing their education are motivated to work even harder when they see how their efforts can really affect the lives of the people positively.

Previously, the concept of a civil learning and democracy has been linked. It is also noted that with the introduction of the civic learning, in some institutions, other than people becoming more involved in their communities, there has also been a sharp increase in voter turnout as people realize they have the ability to change the community in their small way. They also tend to realize one of the most significant ways to make that change is through exercising one's right to vote. Therefore, service learners do not only recognize the importance of voting themselves, but also spread awareness of how something as trivial as casting a vote can make a difference.

How Civic learning in preparing students for non-emergency civic situations

In this section we will establish the link between civic learning and non-emergency civic situations. As discussed earlier, civic learning inculcates a sense of responsibility in students that they need to work for the public welfare and their respective communities. Non-emergency civic situations will provide the opportunity for these students to put their skills to test. The students who undergo civic learning training programs feel that they are responsible for helping the community in every way possible, so when they will be faced by a non-emergency situation they will be motivated to tackle it.

Resolving or helping with non-emergency situations will not only help the students to ease the burden on public servants such as the police, paramedics, etc., but will also help them to help eliminate a threat that a community faces at large.

So let us again look at some real life scenarios and see how a student who has received a civic learning training would handle such a situation as compared to one who has not received a civic training:

Subject A: Civic learning /Community service trainee

Subject B: Random citizen with no civic learning experience

A storm has broken out in the town of Portlandia; as the storm was at a high magnitude of one, that has knocked down the various trees and uprooted traffic signs on the road; a tree has been knocked down on the main freeway, leading to the city and is blocking the road and similarly the stop sign has been removed from the main intersection.

As subject A, passes by the broken tree, the first step is that he identifies that there is a threat that could put the lives of the people of his town in danger. He feels responsible. A normal passerby, such as Subject B, would justify not removing the impediment by presenting the argument that it is not his/her responsibility to remove the tree, rather the municipal authorities' responsibility to do so. It would definitely be an opportunity for Subject A, as he would be looking to help his community in every way possible.

His critical thinking skills would help him make smart decisions about the situation, so when the subject will go to get the equipment to remove the tree, he will make sure to place the traffic cones and diversion signs to warn the drivers to stay away from the danger in the meanwhile. Similarly, his motivation to work for the safety of his community will actually force him to direct the traffic when the situation is being taken care of. Subject A, will also use his writing skills to write to the public authorities or the city council about how these threats could be eradicated in the future, or participate in the discussions in the public forums about how it could have been eliminated, such as fixing the stop signs with the concrete blocks.

Mr. Shawn was in a hit and run accident; his left rear wheel was knocked off and he was abandoned on the roadside. Even before he could reach out to the police to come to his rescue, Subject A, who was alerted about the situation through a mobile application notification, came to Mr. Shawn's rescue. Not only did he help the man out that day, but also testified as a witness for Mr. Shawn when he was registering the report, so the police obtained the camera footage to view who had hit Mr. Shawn's vehicle.

Non-emergency situations like open potholes, nonfunctional traffic signals, and building violations are the types of non-emergency situations that we have discussed before. A student who has undergone civic learning would firstly identify situations that can cause a likely threat to the people of that community; he would feel responsible for these open dangers, as he would consider himself liable if any one of these situations would harm any of his community members. He is most likely to work in his own capacity to solve such an issue and where this won't be possible, he will approach the local municipal authority by writing them a letter to register his complaint or he will use a public forum to force the public authorities to take immediate action regarding the situation.

Non-emergency situations do not require immediate assistance from the police, so they give the people of the community a chance to deliberate on pressing issues. For instance, in an emergency, such as an open pothole, the first and most immediate step that a service learner would take would be to put danger signs and wire around it, so that people are warned about its existence. His next step would be to register a complaint with the local authorities, but his campaign would not end there; he would take the negligence of the authority to a public forum and debate why the local authorities are so careless in their behavior and is likely to suggest that workers ensure that all such dangerous openings are sealed in the future.

A number of non-emergency situations fall under the category of nuiSansce, such as loud parties, graffiti, vandalism, loitering and littering of the public places. The age group that is most actively involved in all these activities or responsible for committing these offences is the teenagers and the youth. Civic learning at the college and school will train the students not to act in this manner, as it is destructive behavior towards their community. When there is a thorough, practical learning, they will engage in the civic participation, these youngsters are bound to realize that their positive actions can bring about a huge difference in their communities. Students who have been engaged in the civil learning programs will also discourage their peers from getting involved in such activities.

When it will come to non-emergency situation such as graffiti and vandalism, the service learners would try to engage others in the community to wash the walls in the town covered with graffiti and also restore parks in the area.

Use of drugs is another non-emergency situation that was pointed out; students who have been engaged in the civic learning and training programs will not only discourage people involved in such offenses but also register complaints against those involved. Instead of relying on emergency services and the police, the people of the community realize that they too have a responsibility towards their people and can handle situations without assistance from emergency service providers.

Civic learning instills the belief of working for the community and for a larger goal than focusing on one's own self. This belief motivates the service learners to look at the non-emergency situations as an opportunity that they can utilize to work for the community in the smallest way possible.

CHAPTER 4

Open311

Understanding Open311: A new channel of public services

What is Open311?

Open311 is a technology that connects users and provides them with open channels of communication for issues that concern public areas and public services. So Open311 basically allows people of an area to track issues that concern public spaces and need the attention of the public service authorities.

When the 311 service was launched it was basically sculpted on the model of 911 emergency service, however, instead of emergency situations, citizens or residents could report a non-emergency situation. In some time, the 311 non-emergency services turned into an open311 network. What made this transformation possible was when the phones that were used to make calls to the 311 service turned into smartphones, which were equipped to perform multiple functions, and had an array of new applications.

In addition, the usage of these smartphones increased, as most individuals became owners of the smartphone technology. Almost simultaneously, the 3G and 4G technology surfaced which enabled people to be connected to the World Wide Web at all times and in all places; all of this eventually resulted in the redesigning of the 311 service provider and it was improved in the Open311 service.

The Open311 service basically replaced one to one communication with the mass communication and made the communication channel asynchronous by use of the internet. So if at first, a resident of a town in Sans Francisco (where Open311 technology is functional and widespread) reported a non-emergency issue such as a broken traffic signal at the main intersection through the 311 service, he would dial 311, register the report with the operator and that would be the end of it. However, now with the Open311 technology that the report is on a public forum and people can exchange information about that very public issue.

It also allows users to add to the provided information that could assist the service providers in some manner, for instance, when a report was registered on a missing stop sign after a storm broke out, a resident who saw the report conveyed that the stop sign that was uprooted had landed in her backyard. The information provided is extremely valuable as it saves the time and the money of the local authorities responsible for restoring the stop sign, and this would have not reached the authorities had it not been for the Open311 system.

The 311 service was originally designed to cater to non-emergency situations such as garbage removal, graffiti, etc. In some cities, this service reduced the cost of the city services and the service was not limited to a non-emergency calls anymore, as information regarding the city services and service requests was also entertained. In addition, it became a channel of communication between the public and the local government, as assistance in reaching the various municipal departments and public offices was also provided.

Information regarding events in the city such as city council meetings, carnivals and big scale football matches could also be sought from the 311 line. The operations of the 311 system are not limited to, providing city services to the users, but also served as a backup for the 911 emergency service. The load on the 911 service was reduced, which obviously resulted in an improvement in the emergency services they provide, as the workload was now divided and matters that didn't require immediate police assistance were now handled by the 311 service.

The value of the 311 system in regards to public service can be judged by the introduction of the service in the Orange County Florida. The operations of the 311 system were not fully available when the county was struck by three hurricanes, but a seven-digit number in place of 311 was present and was reached by thousands of residents who registered demands for post hurricane services. The viability and capability of the 311 service to address civic issues became apparent to the local government after the experience and the 311 service was therefore launched in Orange county Florida officially.

In some cities, the Open311 service is used as a tool to judge the performance of the local government and the civic authorities. The line is used by the citizens to register complaints regarding the performance of the public officials regarding a prevailing public issue. In this way, a platform is provided to the public to register their grievances and it is a way to ensure accountability of the government departments.

The open311 service has been used to in some cities to seek information about the taxes and other such important matters. It is also being used to provide information regarding floods, hurricanes and storms where, the most common queries revolve around the timing and the likelihood of the natural calamity hitting the town and the city, and information regarding precautionary measures that the citizens could undertake.

Unlike the 911 service, the Open311 service did not provide services around the clock and the line was not active 24/7 however, the success of Open311 to handle non-emergency services and the increasing popularity led to the introduction of it being active 24/7. In addition, the introduction of the open311 on the web has made live updates possible, which are available at all times.

One of the foremost advantages of Open311 system is that it has streamlined the reporting and registration of the public issues and complaints. Where at first there were many lines and service providers, for example 2121 was the number contacted to report the traffic problems and complaints, all these service providers were unified under one 311 operations; this did not only result in easy access for the citizens who could register all sorts of complaints through one platform, but also reduced the city services costs, as only one operation began catering to all issues faced by the public.

The Open311 system is improving on a daily basis and being improved to provide all kinds of public services. For instance, the newest development in the city of the Chicago is the use of the system to predict as well as to prevent recurring challenges. In the year 2001, the department of sewer and Sanitation used "water in the basement" reports registered by the local residents to identify areas of heavy flooding and renovating the sewer system in those pinpointed areas. The next summer when a similar flood warning was issued, the sewage authority was already prepared to handle the situation and avoided "water in the basement" reports by already addressing the areas that were most likely to be hit by the heavy flooding.

In some cases the town official are able to get a broader perspective on a prevailing problem by tracking complaints reported on the open311 system, for instance, in case of an outbreak of disease in animals the officials would examine the complaints of dead animals, which enabled them to track the origin of the virus and the magnitude of the effects that it had.

The open311 network is also used to register complaints about drug use or sale of narcotics. All these reports can be forwarded to the police, which could help them curb drug related activities in an area. Not only will this organize the community against drug use, but will also raise awareness on the issue.

As the open311 is being improved every day, there is a potential for more growth and an even larger increase in the scope of the public services provided. In addition to reporting a broken traffic signal, what if the users could also report an intersection that poses a threat to the drivers and could use a stop sign or a traffic light. Residents could become more involved, as they will not only register suggestions such as a new park to be developed in a certain area, but also suggest vacant plots that could be restored to build the park. Not only will the participation of the citizens increase, but they will also feel that their opinion matters and their voices are heard. A more advanced form of a similar service would be to take the input of the citizens in the urban planning processes, which would not only ensure that the demands of the local people are being kept insight, but can also employ the expertise that the local community has to offer. For example, an architect can suggest that it would be more viable to create a certain structure in another area in place of the assigned one, as it would be more practical.

The open311 service could also be used to recruit volunteers in order to help supplement the government workers. For example, volunteers required to manage crowds at the football matches or other such large-scale events. Volunteers from the public can also be recruited to take part in the city drives such as a wash-out project to paint off graffiti on walls and public buildings. In addition, these projects could be initiated through the open311 service as volunteers who would like to help could register through the online portal.

The open311 network, which was only limited to registering reports on non-emergency situations, has seen tremendous growth in the scope of the services offered and the amount of the public services being offered will continue to increase, as the 331 operations also enables civic engagement.

History of 311

As discussed in the book earlier on, the 3-1-1 is a special number that is designed to handle non-emergency services in the United States and Canada. After its launch in the United States of America, the 3-1-1 was increasingly used by the other communities and regions. This section will discuss the history of the open 3-1-1. The section will highlight the history of the 3-1-1 in Chicago and 3-1-1 in Baltimore, Mary Land.

Before the establishment of an open 3-1-1, the communities relied heavily on the 9-1-1 number, which offered citizen assistance in various emergency and non-emergency related situations. The call volume of the 9-1-1 system gradually became harder to maintain and the regulatory bodies decided to establish a system that will serve as a backup or additional system for the 9-1-1 call centers.

The major purpose of creating an open 3-1-1 was to separate the emergency situations from the non-emergency situations. Due to the excessive call load on the 9-1-1 system, many serious emergency calls couldn't get a timely response, which created a need for a separate service that would work as a complete non-emergency service department.

N11 code

The number 3-1-1 follows a sequence of the N11 code, a three-digit telephone number that allows citizens of the United States and North America to reach the local municipal or the non-emergency services. The N11 code was introduced by the U.S. Federal Communications Commission (FCC) as a set of abbreviated phone numbers in 1992.

There are various N11 numbers that are assigned to the various public service departments in the United States and Canada. The commonly used N11 numbers include 2-1-1 for the community information and services, the 3-1-1 for non-emergency services, 4-1-1 for the directory assistance, 5-1-1 for the traffic information and police related non-emergency services, 6-1-1 for the telephone company Telco assistance, 7-1-1 for the TDD relay information and services, 8-1-1 for the public utility location information and 9-1-1 for the emergency services including fire department and police department. These numbers are also known as the abbreviated dialing codes.

In Canada, the three digit numbers are also utilized for the various public services, with the few differences. For example, the number 8-1-1 is used in Canada for the non-emergency health services, in contrast to the United States, where the number is used for the public utility location information.

The N11 code is a part of the digit plan that keeps the numbers from being reused or assigned. The code offers various advantages that include easy access to the phone networks, which are otherwise only accessible through seven-digit telephone number. As discussed earlier in the book, the purpose of the 3-1-1 service is to divert the non-emergency calls from the 9-1-1 center, so the 9-1-1 line can stay open for the emergency calls.

Many cities in the United States and North America use 3-1-1 apps to receive citizens' feedback and comments. In 2010, the open 3-1-1 (an application programming interface) was announced for non-emergency services. Today, there are various 3-1-1 apps (discussed earlier in the book) such as HeyGov! MjePge and SeeClickFix that are increasingly utilized by the citizens to submit their requests and inquiries directly to the government or the regulatory bodies.

In the year 1999, the DOT, U.S. Department of Transportation, filed a request with the idea that there should be a nationwide assignment of N11 codes that could be used by both the state and the local governments to provide the citizens with the transportation and the travel information. The travel information includes the information regarding the road construction, alternative routes in the case of an emergency or a road block and at the accident locations.

According to the DOT's research, there are nearly six million vehicle accidents, around 42,000 deaths on the roads and 5.3 million road accident injuries. According to the research, there are around eleven transportation related numbers in the New York and the Washington that allow citizens to have an accurate travel related information. Most of the travel related information is provided to the citizens through telephone, a primary medium for a non-emergency service.

The origin of 311

According to the various resources, the first 3-1-1 service was implemented in the Baltimore, Maryland, with the help of the Maryland's police department. The service was inaugurated in the 1996 with the purpose of creating something similar to the 9-1-1 service. The service was implemented along with the CRM software developed by the Motorola. To date, some of the largest 3-1-1 operations are conducted in Toronto, North America, where the 3-1-1 services commenced in 2009.

In North America, the 3-1-1 service became a popular non-emergency service when the Canadian radio /television and telecommunication commission introduced and promoted the 3-1-1 service as the municipal service in the late 2004.

Before it was introduced as a municipal service number, the 3-1-1 code was used by the various telecommunication companies as a testing number. In Alberta, the 3-1-1 number was used as the automatic number announcement circuit. This practice was discontinued in the early 2005 after the introduction of a new automatic number announcement circuit represented by the number 958-6111. In the United States, the 3-1-1 number was used as an area code. Most commonly, it was used as an area code in the Bell advertisements that depicted phones.

The various regulatory bodies began to realize the need for a specialized system that could provide a backup for the 9-1-1 services and also serve as a separate public service entity to handle everyday situations. In early 1996, the Federal Communications Commission announced the 3-1-1 service as a non-emergency service.

The 3-1-1 service allowed citizens to report non-emergency situations, such as stray animal complaints, small-scale robbery and loss of electricity, to their local government. The 3-1-1 system gives local governments an important opportunity that allows them to connect to the citizens through the 3-1-1 call center and provide an improved public service.

The 3-1-1 service offers several online systems to provide citizens with a platform where they can directly post their comments and feedback regarding a certain service. In addition, the online services also allow citizens to have inquiries and help regarding various non-emergency situations.

Future of 3-1-1

It is impossible to talk about the history of 3-1-1 and not to discuss its future. 3-1-1 services have increasingly improved over the past few years and they continue to make a progress through the various technological applications. This section will discuss the case of Oracle, a multi-national computer technology corporation. In 2013, an Oracle white paper highlighted the future of 3-1-1, which is discussed below.

Case Study: Oracle creates a complete constituent experience with Oracle CX

9-1-1 is the most commonly used three digit emergency service number used all over America, until the regulatory bodies realized that this number was no longer enough to satisfy the wide ranging needs of the citizens. The non-emergency situations were larger in number than the emergency situations, which created a burden on the 9-1-1 service. Most of the time, many emergency related calls were finding it hard to reach the specific department due to the overload of calls on the line. More importantly, there was no system in place to record and track the calls.

To eliminate this problem, the federal commission came up with the idea of non-emergency services that would work separately from the 9-1-1 service, to provide a better public service. In the earlier days, the 3-1-1 service focused on the simple telephone calls and the number tracking systems to handle the non-emergency situations. Today, the 3-1-1 service is more refined and more effective as compared to the early 3-1-1 service. Technological advancements have contributed positively towards the development of the 3-1-1 service, elevating the rate of the success in the various public service departments.

For example, with the help of CRM and advanced tracking systems, local police departments are able to predict the crime patterns, which is a great way to eliminate crime. In the recent years, the crime rates in the major cities have significantly reduced due to the advanced crime pattern analysis that keeps police departments up-to-date, regarding the local crimes such as drug dealing, prostitution and theft.

Local governments realized that the non-emergency service, 3-1-1, can be a great opportunity for constituting to experience the local government. By looking at the recent statistics and research, it can be easily said that the 3-1-1 systems can help the local governments improve a city's condition and create a safer environment for its citizens.

The next generation of non-emergency government solutions

Oracle's CX is a multi-purpose, cloud enabled, customer experience solution that is used in many industries to achieve the customer satisfaction. The 3-1-1 non-emergency services can be greatly influenced by this system, in a way that public service departments can use up-to-date, modern technology to improve the quality of their services.

Local governments can use the new CX for identifying the opportunities that can collectively increase the citizens' satisfaction, regarding various non-emergency situations. The main objectives of the CX are:

- To analyze policy trends and outcomes
- To achieve operational efficiency
- To track the performance of different tasks and activities and to improve the effectiveness of the tasks.

Oracle understands the need of the local governments to access information in a timely fashion. This is why the company offers a complete, reliable solution that will allow 3-1-1 representatives and agents to provide a consistent and an accurate information to the citizens.

311 services

We hope by now you have fully understood the concept of the 3-1-1 service and its various aspects. This section will highlight the various services that are offered through the 3-1-1 service. We will also look at a detailed example of a 3-1-1 service to help you understand the concept better.

What are 3-1-1 services?

As we know, a 3-1-1 service is a non-emergency service that offers citizens timely support for situations that are not strictly serious in nature. In other words, non-emergency services refer to the services that do not need tremendous attention. For example, snow and ice problems in Chicago are non-emergency services. On the other hand, the stray animal problem in New York is a non-emergency situation.

The non-emergency services include animal control, roadway cleanliness, illegal burning, installation of a new street lamps, traffic lights and parking meters, noise complaints, neighborhood complaints, small-scale robbery, utility holes, potholes and sinkholes on the roads, abandoned and stolen vehicle issues and the parking law enforcement, to name a few.

Here it is important to mention that the 3-1-1 service does not act alone. In other words, it is a centralized public service system that is designed with the consolidation of various other public service departments including the police department and the fire department. For those who find it hard to understand how 3-1-1 works, here is a brief description of the system.

The 3-1-1 service system is integrated with the various local government and the service departments. Whenever a citizen files a complaint or requests the information regarding a road accident, the 3-1-1 representative transfers the call to the subject matter experts; not every CSA is trained to handle all kinds of non-emergency situations. So, all the departments coordinate to provide a solution for a non-emergency situation. This not only helps the citizens to get a quick response, but also helps government departments to focus on their job rather than dealing with unrelated calls.

According to Kristin Gonzenbach, the Director of Process Improvement, Dekalb County, GA, *"If we can reduce someone's call volume by 50%, that's four hours a day that they can now spend doing what they were hired to do. Efficiency gains are exponential at that point."*

3-1-1 for Cities

Now, you know what the most prominent nonemergency services are and how the 3-1-1 service system works to eliminate a non-emergency related problems from the city. The 3-1-1 services are always improving. Quite recently, the Obama administration introduced the '3-1-1 for cities' program as a part of the network (national resource network). The program '3-1-1 for cities' will allow citizens to have a direct access to the panel of experts who will provide insightful information regarding various economical and development related issues.

This program will greatly help small and large-scale business owners who are always looking for an expert's advice regarding the economic conditions. The experts will be able to provide solid strategies and solutions to the current economic problems, to help the local governments manage the cities better.

The network has direct partnerships with the local government officials, such as mayors, city management and the local leaders, that offer government officials ample resources so that every single local government unit can contribute positively towards the economic growth of the country and prosperity of the citizens.

The network established, according to the demand of various city officials, throughout the country for a direct access to the experts who can provide assistance and information regarding various economic issues. Through the national resource network, more than 50 cities have access to the '3-1-1 for Cities.' Now, citizens can have a direct access to the expert assistance through the national resource network. The network can be reached through www. nationalresourcenetwork.org.

Example of 3-1-1 service

This section will discuss the example of housing inspections through the 3-1-1 call center. The section will highlight the complaint process and case development of the housing inspection complaints that are placed to 3-1-1.

Housing Inspections

Housing inspections are one of the most prominent services provided through the 3-1-1 service. By law, the property owners are required to keep their house surroundings clean to promote public health safety. Citizens can file complaints against other citizens who fail to abide by these rules.

The Complaint Process

The housing inspections are handled by the regulatory services, housing inspections division. The department handles the complaints regarding the poor hygienic conditions of the properties. The department handles the property hygiene issues in two ways. First, the citizens file the complaint against a certain property owner and the division proactively gets involved in the process and makes sure that the issue are resolved. Secondly, the division's representatives, or agents, monitor different areas and identify the properties that are kept unclean.

The citizens can file a complaint through the 3-1-1 service, which is immediately entered into the Frontlink application and the complaint is transferred to the KIVA interface that issues the work order. It is important to remember here that only the citizen-reported complaints are entered in the Frontlink application. Division-related complaints are entered into the KIVA interface via the division inspectors. The cases entered by the division inspectors are not entered into the frontlink as citizen entered the complaints.

The KIVA application sends warning letters to the certain property owners regarding the housing conditions. The application continuously tracks housing conditions and sends re-inspection warning letters to the property owners. The application tracks different housing inspection cases through the housing inspection enforcement process.

Case Development

- The complaints reported to the 3-1-1 call center are immediately entered to the Frontlink and are interfaced to KIVA for immediate storage.
- The complaints are processed through a batch and stored in a KIVA database, for further processing. The complainants with incomplete information are rejected and then re-entered for reprocessing.
- The next day, the KIVA application generates work orders for the division inspectors. The inspectors work on the work order in the KIVA application and update the status of the work order in the Frontlink. The Frontlink updates also go through the batch process every day.
- The housing inspection cases remain open in the Frontlink and KIVA application, as long as the issue remains unresolved. Once the inspectors update the application regarding the application process, the case is closed in both the KIVA and the Frontlink.

Availability of 3-1-1 services

The launch of the 3-1-1 service revolutionized the public service sector of the industry. Before 3-1-1, the only open telephone line for both non-emergency and emergency services was 9-1-1. The 3-1-1 service not only took the load off of the 9-1-1 service, but also provided the various opportunities for the local governments to create a healthy environment for the citizens.

According to a survey report, more than fifty to sixty percent of the non-emergency calls were placed to 9-1-1 before the launch of the 3-1-1 service, which caused inefficiencies in the government agencies, as it was impossible to maintain a huge volume of both the non-emergency and the emergency calls.

The 3-1-1 service was introduced in the mid 90's to separate the two departments—emergency services and the non-emergency services. To make sure that the 3-1-1 service was easily accessible, the government officials created several marketing campaigns to educate the citizens about the service and its benefits. A few years after the launch of the 3-1-1 service, citizens were still placing emergency calls to 3-1-1. The local government addressed the issue through extensive marketing and educational campaigns that eliminated the issue to some extent. Today, citizens still place the emergency calls to 3-1-1 and non-emergency calls to 9-1-1.

For further rectification, the local governments have consolidated the two service departments in a way that the two departments continuously collaborate to identify the non-emergency and emergency calls, and forward them to the respective departments.

Since its launch, the 3-1-1 service has been available to every citizen in the United States and North America. The 3-1-1 service can be reached through telephone, email and through the 3-1-1 website www.open311.org.

3-1-1 is regarded as a feasible solution for inquiry and help, as compared to the seven digit numbers that are hard to remember.

Making 3-1-1 Available

Before the launch of the 3-1-1 service in various cities, the city officials and regulatory bodies arranged a thorough marketing and education plan to create a public awareness. The use of three digit numbers as an emergency number was started in the early 90's, mainly for the reason that they are easy to remember and do not get assigned. The 3-1-1 service is easy to access as citizens can use a telephone, online service or directly walk into the call center to report a complaint or ask for assistance. Even in the smaller cities, the 3-1-1 service proactively works to eliminate the citizens' non-emergency issues.

The service is mainly made available through telephone. The citizens can dial 3-1-1 and report a complaint to the CSA. If the complaint is not related to the department, it will be transferred to the relevant department within a few minutes. In addition, the 3-1-1 service is made available to the citizens through the online service that allow citizens to record their complaints or ask for an assistance, regarding various non-emergency issues. Citizens can also use web mail to reach the 3-1-1 representatives.

In cities like Los Alamos County and New Mexico, most citizens prefer directly contacting a 3-1-1 service representative rather than using the online service. According to a research study, fifty seven percent of the citizens contact the 3-1-1 representatives through telephone and about thirty seven percent of the citizens walk into their nearest 3-1-1 centers to file a complaint, or receive assistance with an inquiry. The research has found that few people utilize the online service; however, many people visit the 3-1-1 website for information regarding different services.

Staffing and Employee Training before launching 3-1-1 service

Before the 3-1-1 service is made available to the citizens, the city officials conduct an extensive training program for the employees and the staff members who will become the customer service representatives. The training of the staff members is the most crucial part of the implementation process, as the representatives should be prepared for every kind of a non-emergency situation.

There are two groups of employees who work at the 3-1-1 call center. The first group represents the first line representatives that interact with the citizens. The second group of staff members includes the subject matter experts that excel in various non-emergency related topics. They are the individuals who provide in-depth assistance to the citizens who require a specific information.

Generally, both groups are provided with the initial training before they are moved to their specific departments and are trained individually. The subject matter experts specialize in various non-emergency related subjects such as domestic violence, property disputes, construction licenses and permits and other subject matters that require specialized assistance.

The first group or the call center agents, on the other hand, are trained to understand the different operations of various local government departments, in order to provide an accurate assistance to the citizens. This part of the training helps agents to better understand the day-to-day activities of the local government agencies and explain the processes to the citizens in a comprehensive way.

In addition, some of the center agents are also trained as 9-1-1 dispatchers for the national emergency situations. As mentioned before, every 3-1-1 center acts as backup for the 9-1-1 center, which in the training part, constituted various modules train specific groups of staff members regarding the emergency situations that might occur.

The staff members are not the only individuals that are trained before the 3-1-1 service is launched. The local government departments are also trained so that they can make use of the 311/CRM and learn to use the application for a better coordination and operation.

Example of Staff Training in various Jurisdictions

The training of the staff members is done according to the rules, regulations and procedures of the county and the state. 3-1-1 call centers in different states of the United States of America operate through their own local laws and regulations. For example, in Dekalb County, Georgia, the 3-1-1 call center provides county services and, therefore, the training of the staff members is done in an institutionalized or formal manner. The formal training takes about 3 weeks.

Similarly, in Louisville, Kentucky, the 3-1-1 call centers provide a city services. Therefore, the employees are trained in-house with the help of outsourced trainers. The in-house training takes about six to eight weeks.

Consider another example of Miami-Dade County, Florida. The 3-1-1 center in this county offers both city and county services. Therefore, employees are trained in a formal, institutionalized manner. The training takes about six to seven weeks.

The training of the staff members or agents is one of the most crucial things. If the 3-1-1 service is made available without any proper training of the employees, it can result in unsatisfied citizens and less efficient public services. Therefore, all the major cities in the United States and North America provided extensive training to their 3-1-1 call center employees before they made the service available to the public.

In what cities 3-1-1 service is available?

3-1-1 in the United States

As mentioned before, the 3-1-1 service is available in all the major cities of the United States and North America. In the United states, the service is available in Austin, Texas; Albuquerque, New Mexico; Akron, Ohio; Chattanooga, Tennessee; Fort Wayne, Indiana; Buffalo, New York; Denver, Colorado; Detroit, Michigan;

Hampton, Virginia; Evanston, Illinois; Las Vegas, Nevada; Kansas City, Missouri; Indianapolis, Indiana; Philadelphia, Pennsylvania; Little Rock, Arkansas; New York City, New York Riverside, California; Orange County, Florida; Knoxville, Tennessee; Seattle and Washington; Springfield,

In North America, the 3-1-1 service is available in major cities including Fort St. John, British Columbia; Calgary, Alberta; Greater Sudbury, Ontario; Halifax Regional Municipality, Nova Scotia; Edmonton, Alberta; Gatineau, Quebec; Regional Municipality of Peel, Ontario; Halton Region, Ontario; Ottawa, Ontario; Laval, Quebec; Montreal, Quebec; St. John's, Newfoundland and Labrador; Montreal, Quebec; Toronto, Ontario; Vancouver, British Columbia; Winnipeg, Manitoba and Windsor, Ontario.

3-1-1 in Europe

Many European countries use a non-emergency service and various others adopting the concept. In Sweden, the emergency service can be reached through 114 14. The calls placed through this number are usually charged at the same rate as other seven or ten digit numbers. In Finland, the emergency service can be reached through 112. Quite recently, Finland's regulatory bodies introduced a new number for emergency purposes, which is represented by 116 115. Calls placed to this number are free of charge. In Germany, the emergency and non-emergency services can be reached through 115.

3-1-1 in the United Kingdom

The UK government has created a plan to implement a single number, 101, for the local police departments, so that they can coordinate better to resolve crime related emergency issues. The citizens can use the number to reach the local police department for non-emergency related crime situations.

3-1-1 for Homeland Security

Over the years, government officials have realized that the 3-1-1 service can do much more than just handle the non-emergency services requested by the citizens. The major benefit of the service is its contribution towards homeland security. As mentioned earlier in the book, the 3-1-1 service system utilizes CRM software to track, the identity and addresses of the various callers, which allows the system to create a complete database of citizens' profiles.

These profiles can be used when determining the crime patterns in the specific region. In addition, 3-1-1 is a great tool for citizens to communicate with the city authorities. Citizens can easily report suspicious activity or an individual by simply calling the 3-1-1 center. The 3-1-1 center representative will forward the call to the specific security department for the immediate processing of the request or the report.

The consolidation of the different government agencies, including the police department, plays a great role in protecting the city from the foreign bodies that intend to create disruption in the city.

To create a protective wall against the suspicious activities, the local governments have integrated 3-1-1 centers with the 9-1-1 centers. In many cities, the 3-1-1 call centers are designed to operate as 9-1-1 dispatch workstations that are of great use in case of the national emergencies.

Nearly half of the 3-1-1 centers in all the cities are designed to operate as 9-1-1 workstations for the emergency situations. The purpose of designing 3-1-1 systems to operate as 9-1-1 dispatch centers is to create a backup system that can be immediately utilized in case of national emergencies.

Moreover, many of the CSAs or 3-1-1 call center agents and representatives are trained as 9-1-1 agents who are specialized in taking emergency reports. The local government consistently educates citizens regarding the use of non-emergency services, to make sure that every citizen has ample information regarding the emergency services.

Usage of 3-1-1 services

As we have discussed earlier in the book, the 3-1-1 call center serves wide ranging purposes. It is consolidated with the different local governments and the public service departments to create an increased efficiency. Before we go any further, let's differentiate between the 9-1-1 and the 3-1-1 services. You probably know the difference between the two, but to make it clearer, let's briefly go through about both the services in which situation it can be used.

3-1-1 vs. 9-1-1

Use 9-1-1 services only when you require a quick response from the fire, police and health departments. For example, use 9-1-1 for serious health related issues, residential or building fires and serious crime activity (crime activity that threatens homeland security).

On the other hand, use 3-1-1 services only when you have a non-emergency situation. Some people are usually confused about the definition of a non-emergency situation. For those who can't wrap their heads around the concept of non-emergency services; a non-emergency situation is one that is not life threatening or does not include large-scale criminal activity.

In other words, if you think that the crime or suspicious activity does not threaten your homeland security, place a call to 3-1-1. Similarly, if the suspicious activity seems to be dangerous enough to cause homeland breach, call 9-1-1.

Call 3-1-1 only when you need:

- Assistance with a non-emergency situation
- Information about the city
- Information about the shelter homes
- Emergency numbers for fire, health or police departments

We hope that clarifies all the confusions about the two services. In the next section, we will discuss the benefits of using the 3-1-1 service, with examples, to help you grasp the concept better.

The Benefits of Implementing the 3-1-1 Service

All the major cities in the United States and North America have 3-1-1 call centers. After the inauguration of the 3-1-1 call center in Baltimore, Maryland, various cities adopted the concept and today, there are dozens of call centers in each state of the Unites States of America. Before we move to the examples, let's briefly discuss the major benefits of the 3-1-1 service:

- The major benefit of implementing the 3-1-1 call center is improved homeland security. As discussed above, 3-1-1 call centers are incorporated with various other local government departments, including the police department, which allows regulatory bodies to keep an eye on the suspicious activities.

According to Ed Harris, the deputy director of the Austin Police department, *"3-1-1 has been a miracle. It has been a godsend for us. 3-1-1 saved us not only from having our 9-1-1 system swamped, but saved our citizens who had true emergencies, such as heart attacks and crimes in progress, from getting a busy signal."*[17]

- The 3-1-1 call centers provide a backup center for the 9-1-1 center for the national emergencies. For example, in the event of a

---

[17] Building a 3-1-1 System for Police Non-Emergency Calls: A Process and Impact Evaluation, Austin Police Department

natural disaster, such as Hurricane Katrina, various, 3-1-1 workstations are used as 9-1-1 workstations.

- The 3-1-1 service allows citizens to get a quicker response, which was never possible before. Due to the heavy load of both emergency and non-emergency calls on a single center, the local public service departments were not able to assist with everything.

Examples

In Baltimore, the 3-1-1 service work in conjunction with the city's CitiStat service, reducing the city costs by a significant level. Many municipal officers recommend government officials to implement the 3-1-1 service, along with the installation of CitiStat. CitiStat provides a strong infrastructure to record and forward the service requests placed by the citizens through the 3-1-1 service.

Orange County, Florida, has been struck with various hurricanes in the past few years. During the implementation of the 3-1-1 service in the Orange County, the city experienced three major hurricanes. The 3-1-1 service was used through the six digit number 836-3-1-11, which received countless post hurricane services requests.

In Philadelphia, the 3-1-1 service was implemented in the year 2008. Since then, the service has helped citizens with resourceful information regarding the city. In addition, the Philadelphia 3-1-1 call center has also helped citizens with graffiti removal, clogged drains, housing inspections, stray dogs and other animals, and other non-emergency situations.

Frequently Asked Questions about 3-1-1 service

Most people are confused about various aspects of the 3-1-1 service center. Most people do not know how to find the right department or how to reach the 3-1-1 center in case their cellular service fails to connect them. This section attempts to answer the frequently asked questions that most citizens have in their mind.

- Whom do I speak to when I call 3-1-1?

    Your call is received by a highly trained representative, also known as the customer service representative (CSA). The 3-1-1 customer service representatives are highly specialized individuals that can help you out with any non-emergency situation.

- How do I know I have reached the right department?

    The representative of the call center will let you know if you have reached the right department. In most cases, the representative can handle any kind of non-emergency situation. If, in case, the representative is unable to provide you with assistance, regarding your non-emergency situation, your call will be forwarded to the subject matter expert. If you would like to reach the fire, health or police department, you will have the option to route to the 9-1-1 center.

- What if I am unable to place a call to 3-1-1?

  Generally, all business and cellular services are connected with the 3-1-1 center. However, you may not be able to reach a 3-1-1 center if you are calling from outside your district or a city. In case you are unable to reach 3-1-1 center, place a call to (202) 737-4404 and reach the citywide service center.

- How do I track the progress of my request?

  After you place a request or complaint through the 3-1-1 call center, you will be given a tracking number, which will help you track the progress of your request. To track the progress of your request, create an online account on the 3-1-1 website or contact a customer service representative to have an update regarding your request.

- Can my request still be tracked if I lose the tracking number?

  Yes, your request can be tracked through the phone number, home address or email address that you have provided at the time of placing your request with the call center.

- What type of issues can I report online?

  You can report any kind of non-emergency situation. The most common services, offered through the 3-1-1 service, include housing inspections, animal control, suspicious activity report, sidewalk snow and licensing and permit issuance, to name a few.

- What if I don't get a timely response?

  It is highly unlikely that you will not get a timely response. However, if that happens, you can contact your nearest 3-1-1 center and ask for the reason for the delay.

- When should I call 3-1-1

  You should only call 3-1-1 when you need assistance with non-emergency situations or need to report crime activity like drug dealing and prostitution. Other than that, you can contact the 3-1-1 call center for abandoned automobiles, parking enforcement, illegal garbage dumping, street light and signal light repair, broken meters and for additional information regarding the city services.

Tips for Reporting a Complaint or a Suspicious Activity

Many people avoid reporting suspicious activity, mainly because they believe that they might get dragged into the case. This section offers some practical tips that can help you eliminate this fear while making the streets safe for everybody.

- If you are reporting suspicious activity to the 3-1-1 representative, then it is better to do so anonymously. Information easily leaks and there is a good chance that the people about whom you are placing the complaint will find out.

- Always ask the customer service representative to keep your information confidential. If you are placing a request of a street lamp repair, then there is no harm in giving your name and other personal information. However, in case you are filing for a complaint, it is better to be careful.

- Always provide accurate information to the customer service representative. The representatives have a huge database of citizens' profiles and sometimes, it is not possible to find the right address if you have provided incomplete information. For example, house number 456 near East Oakland is not an accurate address. House 456, street 36, East Oakland is an accurate address.

- Always give a short description of the issue for which you are filing a complaint. Let the customer representative know why a certain issue needs to be taken seriously. For example, if you have noticed drug-dealing activity in your neighborhood, provide details of the activity to the customer service representative.

Also describe the individuals involved, and the extent of the activity.

- Always let the representative know about the seriousness of the situation. For example, was the suspicious person in your church, neighborhood or workplace? In addition, let the representative know how the agencies can locate the suspicious person. For example, if you notice a suspicious individual in your neighborhood, describe his attire or anything that could help the customer service representative.

By following the above-mentioned tips you can keep yourself safe while contributing towards the well-being of your society.

The open model

Let us look at the open311 model more closely and bring our focus to the key term, which is "open." At present, the most important function of the open311 technology is to report and track issues concerning public spaces. Of these issues, the majority fall under the category of non-emergency situations such as open potholes, graffiti, vandalism, littering in the public spaces and broken streetlights or traffic signals, as well as all other issues that concern public buildings and infrastructure.

A resident of a particular area will use his mobile phone or computer device to enter information or register a report- usually a photo is uploaded, about a problem at a given location. This report is then forwarded to the relevant authorities so that they can address the issues at hand. How the open model differs is that the report registered is available for anyone to see. In addition, anybody can contribute more information regarding the report. The open model encourages the community to get more involved in the issues of the community and brings people together. It also allows the residents of a town or city to work in collaboration with the government authorities; therefore, it acts as a channel of communication between the people and the municipal government.

This engagement develops the trust of the people. The open311 also ensures transparency and accountability; as the issue is reports on a public forum, it allows everyone to view the progress of the local government and their municipal authorities. For instance, if a report for a broken streetlight is registered and even after months, no step has been taken by the responsible authorities to fix it, the people will question the respective government over their mismanagement. The system also ensures transparency and this as a result encourages participation of the public in civic matters.

Due to the ever increasing popularity of the Open311 service many people developed applications in relation to the Open311 on their own, but the drawback of applications being built independently was that all these applications were not connected, hence their services were limited to a single city. This posed a major impediment not only when it came into usage, but also developers faced difficulties. To tackle this problem many cities that offer Open311 services have started to use APIs or Application Programming interfaces to allow deeper access to the data resources.

The use of Application Programming Interfaces has improved the whole system as the data uploaded by any individual is not just available for reading or viewing, but the users can also record queries regarding the live data feed and they have the option to submit new information. This new API system allows open311 application and mash-ups to fully engage with a city's 311 system. However, to provide interoperability, the Open311 system has to be unified by the means of a common language or standard protocol. This can happen if developers turn their focus from including different requirements for each city to access data in developing new features of the application. This would make the user's life very simple, as they would be able to use the same application to reach out to the Open311 system all across the globe. In addition all users can benefit from new innovative features that are added on a common ground.

This is how the "open" model has been built, not only does it allow access to the data resources to all the members of the public, but also allows the users to openly participate by giving them the power to comment on a Newsfeed related to any update or report concerning a public issue. With the open model not even a speck of the information uploaded is hidden. This ensures complete transparency, encourages the participation of the general public and increases the collaboration of citizens and the government authority.

With new developments a user has been enabled to access any data and can also compare what scope of services each city provides by making a comparison through which they could make a constructive suggestions on how to improve the existing Open311 services in their city.

Open311 pattern

Open311 is a form of e-governance; the Open311 is not only putting a lot of data out on the web but is also making use of an interface such as http to expose the data to the maximum number of people. However, the real success of Open311 will not be dependent on how much data is put out there, but on how that data could positively benefit the society. The primary purpose of the open trend is that technology developers, as well as the users, can use the public data to create applications that could bring light to various public issues and at the same time, ensure transparency and accountability of the local government systems.

To understand the Open pattern better, let us review the example of Catherine, who sees a broken tree on the road in the city Boston, where she lives. She would like to know if the issue has been reported and if it has not been, to report it. When Catherine is in Boston she would like to know what services the government offers and when she moves to Aberdeen in Scotland, she still remains equally concerned about the public issue and wants to go ahead and report it.

In short, Catherine wants to access a common capability across different data contexts, which in this case would be the different cities. This is where the pattern comes in, which is the workflow of an abstract application addressing the common capability that is the public issue, by removing small details such as the location and parameterizing the API calls. The open pattern is very valuable because it standardizes the usage experience, as the user behavior remains similar, for instance, it allows Catherine to report the same problem which she shows great concern for, even when she is in a different continent. For the technology developers the development becomes simpler because it enables them to templatize API interactions.

Now we must link all this information regarding the value of open pattern to the example of Catherine for better comprehension. The first step would be, Catherine is buying and downloading the application and launching a sub-application and choosing the city she is in. She will then continue by selecting a category around which the services of the city are grouped, for example health, traffic, and infrastructure. She will then find the list of the services offered concerning the said issue and will also be able to look at the agencies involved which provide the services. More than one agency could be offering services for a single category such as health. Then Catherine would be notified if that were the case. By being fixed on a single category and choosing different cities, Catherine can also compare the level and scope of service provided in different cities.

The pattern concept is supported by the cloud based platform and only this type of networking can make the pattern operational. Cloud based platform is basically a form of an internet based computing, in which a large number of remote servers that are connected, allow the centralized data storage and online access to resources. The Pattern is a template for an application, it may contain deployable assets, service dependencies and configurable properties.

The process of registering the pattern and making use of the pattern is quite basic. A portal is used for registration of the pattern and all the information regarding the pattern, such as deployable assets and configurable properties, are also recorded. A future user discovers the pattern on the portal, based on the scenario of interest and explores its configuration points. The portal also shows all the APIs that is registered on it and can be used to instantiate the pattern. The user selects the pattern, configures and automatically generates an instance, and deploys the instantiated pattern. The application is now available for use like any other web application. At a later stage, the deployed application can be destroyed as desired.

The open model and pattern will enable the maximum number of users to get involved in addressing public issues and increase civic participation. In addition, it will enable the developers to create a new and innovative features that will ultimately increase the scope of the services offered and will also increase the usage and participation. As the open model and pattern ensures transparency, accountability, as well as collaboration, it will lead to the strengthening of the democratic government system at the grass root level. The open system will also support the idea of the world being a global village, as the services would be made available to all citizens around the globe.

Open311 API

In the simplest terms, Open311 API (application programming interface) is an instrument, through which the inhabitants of a city can deliver their requests and reports of public concerns and their locations, along with any other details possible, directly to a server with a database, in the form of a call for action. This organized and easy to decipher database is then accessed by the relevant authorities or governing body who then efficiently address each request for service. It is an open standard developed by the organization named 'OpenPlans'.

OpenPlans is a technology centered, nonprofit organization which aims to make the government a more accessible institution for the general public. Open311 is the next step in the evolution of the traditional phone-based 311 services. The conventional method of reporting an issue to the authorities revolved around a one-to-one interaction between the citizen and the establishment, mostly through the medium of phone calls. But with the help of the free web services of Open311, a number of different people can simultaneously and freely exchange information about any social issue they want.

Since Open311 is a relatively fresh API, it does not host a large extent of services. Currently, it is frequently being used for the reporting and tracking of non-emergency issues in communities. Non-emergency issues can be defined as situations in which there is no immediate threat to an individual's life or safety. Most of the concerns that are reported on Open311 revolve around public spaces and infrastructure. Examples of commonly reported problems are potholes on roads, damaged buildings, pollution caused by littering, vandalism and broken traffic or street lights.

Since Open311 is accessible through mobile devices or computers, the first step to know how it operates is that an individual can use their technology to enter information about a specific public concern, along with any other details or photographs possible. A report is then formed out of all this information and routed to the respective authorities, who then address the problem at the earliest possible time.

Apart from being a many-to-many asynchronous form of communication, Open311 has many other significant distinctions from the conventional 311 report mechanism. As Open 11 is an open model, the information is readily available for anyone in the city to access, similarly, there are no restrictions imposed on who can contribute to its database. Such convenient and nonrestrictive access makes collecting and organizing information on a large scale much more convenient. Not only is Open311 a handy platform, it also brings to the forefront issues that need immediate attention from the local authorities.

As the database is open to the public access and viewing, it provides a new level of transparency and simultaneously increases the accountability of the officials responsible for mitigating the problems reported. The transparency and accountability assured with Open311 guarantees that every citizen's voice is heard. As this platform ensures results in the form of public concerns being addressed swiftly by the authorities, participation in aid of the provision of non-emergency civic services is also encouraged.

Even though the development of Open311 is relatively recent, it already has access to a number of servers. To facilitate comprehension, a server is defined as a computer or a program which facilitates and manages access to a centralized source or service in a network. The servers on Open311 range from FixMyStreet, which is used to report common potholes and broken streetlight problems in the streets, to servers like FixMyTransport, which helps people report their transport problems and signal for help. The services of Open311 are currently present mostly in North America as well as in some parts of Germany, Finland, Canada and Portugal.

There are several benefits associated with using an open standard like Open311. Firstly, it is a simple method of communication that can be implemented by just about anyone, without the need of getting special permission to access or without using any money to pay for it; chiefly, it is free technology. Another upside to this technology is that once the knowledge of an open standard spread and different technology systems start incorporating them in their systems, a variety of systems from different manufacturers can interact with each other. In simple terms, whoever a person is interacting with does not need to have the same system or brand.

This is good news for the governing body of any city or community because essentially it means that if their database is open for access to the outside world, all the reports coming from a multitude of different sources all end up on one platform and system, as opposed to being on many different websites or applications. This is because the traditional systems used for the purpose of reporting social issues had not been programmed to speak a common language with the public. Most often, this was done on purpose by the suppliers of such systems so that the part being used by them would have to be paid separately for any new channel or server they wished to add.

As a solution, Open311 not only lowers the government's costs, but also rescues them from the suppliers' expensive traps of upgrades for systems. This makes data handling much easier and also makes the process of addressing the public concerns a much smoother one for the authorities, not to mention that it ensures results.

The current services provided by Open311, essentially limit to being a model that serves to address the non-emergency issues. Not to undermine the significance of non-emergency services, Open311 can also be used to track and report other central issues that revolve around the emergency situations like floods and earthquakes. In fact, there is already a system named Ushahidi that uses the same open standard model used by Open311, which aided immensely in the rescue and relief work done after the disastrous earthquake in Haiti in 2010.

The existing functions provided by Open311 are only the beginning of the amount of the civic engagement activities that can be facilitated and encouraged by such technologies. There is a whole unexplored future of the various applications of such an open standard system. If developed further, instead of the limited reporting and tracking function provided by the Open311, currently, it can also be used to raise awareness and manage various volunteer efforts to aid the government and its workers in the civic services and the community development.

A lot of people have been inspired by the myriad of possibilities and potential brought forth by the open model of Open311. This inspiration has led to the development of a variety of different applications that have been built on the framework of open standards. The new applications are mostly compatible with the system of Open311. For example, there are many different cities that have built their own open standard iPhone applications that are compatible with the 311 services. But there is one drawback to the outbreak of the development of different open standard applications.

The new independent applications cannot function together on a common platform and are designed specifically for a particular city, making them inoperable in other cities. This vastly diminishes the effectiveness and usefulness of these applications, but this is not a discouraging reality as to time, continued research and developmental efforts, all such issues will eventually be resolved.

Recently, in order to encourage and promote higher levels of civic engagement, governments have launched a number of initiatives. Most of these initiatives revolve around opening of the data reports on 311 servers to citizens so they can analyze them and proactively offer solutions as well. Keeping in mind the range of benefits of the open standard system of Open311, it is an essential innovation in encouraging civic engagement and empowering citizens to make a difference in not only their own society, but also possibly to the world.

Not only that, but Open311 also makes the task of governance a more inclusive and smarter activity, rendering it an irreplaceable tool. But it has not yet reached the stage where it does not require updates and improvements in its software and is still yet to be perfected.

APIs and the Growth of Cloud Based Technologies

No software is capable of functioning independently without relying on some other software's help to complete its functions. To accomplish the task of requesting the services of separate software, the asking program utilizes a set of standardized requests, which are formally known as application programming interfaces (APIs). The APIs are a set of standardized instructions that are easily understood by the request receiving the program and have two benefits. Firstly, APIs ensures simplification by providing an easier language that hides complexity and secondly, they provide standardization.

Almost every existing software or application critically depends on these APIs, even with regards to performing a function as basic as accessing a file from a database. The use of APIs by applications and software is not entirely a novel idea as even desktop computers and laptops employs APIs to move information between different programs. An example of how APIs facilitate the function of different programs is when Microsoft word interacts with a printer, sending it different commands and instructions.

Due to the use of APIs, Microsoft Word does not need to know what kind of a printer is being used and the printer carries out Microsoft Word's instructions efficiently. On the internet, APIs facilitate the cooperative functions of services like Google Maps and ultimately results in enabling them to 'rent out' their services to other applications and programs.

The process through which APIs facilitate the interaction between two programs can be outlined as the APIs revealing the details regarding some of a programs function in the computerized world. This enables other applications to share the data and perform services on the behalf of another application, without making a developer go through the hassle of revealing all of the software's codes. It also allows program developers to employ a set of predefined functions, instead of writing the standardized instructions from scratch, resulting in the smooth interaction of different applications within an operating system.

If a developer were to make public all of a program coding, it would be a tedious task resulting in no additions to inefficiency. When used correctly, APIs make it possible for an application and program developers to mix and match APIs for existing applications to produce various new applications and services.

There are different sets of APIs for all the diverse types of operating systems like Windows, Mac and UNIX. Furthermore, APIs are also used by gaming consoles and every other category of hardware devices that can employ software programs. APIs not only make the programmer's job easier, they also make it easier for the program user to navigate an application as the APIs ensure that all the programs using the same APIs have analogous user interfaces. These different types of APIs include Web service APIs, WebSocket APIs, Library-based APIs, Class-based APIs, Object remoting APIs, Hardware APIs and Operating Software functions and routines.

A web service API is a software that enables access to its services through an address, known as a URL, on what is known as the World Wide Web. The web service offers information in the format that other applications can comprehend and use. In library-based APIs, an application imports a library of codes or binary functions and uses them to perform many different actions and exchange of information. Similarly, class-based APIs are a special type of library-based APIs. Class-based APIs define instructions in object-oriented languages which are organized around the specific classes.

Each class offers a set of information and behaviors that corresponds to how humans understand a concept. Similarly, the operating systems (OS) that we routinely use every day to perform many different functions on our desktops and laptops are also based on APIs that facilitate the interaction of software programs with the OS. For example, it facilitates functions like accessing a file system, displaying the content of a file on the screen, error notifications, etc. The other types of APIs also employ similar techniques.

There have been many instances where the availability of APIs has led to the shutdown of applications that were favorites. A well-known example is that of, when Twitter restricted the third party application use of its APIs which destroyed numerous alternative Twitter clients, and left users with no choice but to stick to the applications provided solely by the Twitter itself. This allowed twitter to form a monopoly out of its services and was justified by Twitter as a move that was necessary to ensure a unique Twitter experience.

There are many other similar examples of restricted APIs and the shutdown of client services, but they have not discouraged the enthusiasm of developers, of the benefits derived from the use of APIs. Similarly, users back APIs as they open to them a world of many different clients-based applications and services.

The success of APIs has brought about the emergence of API management. API management means any process that includes publishing, promoting or overseeing APIs in a safe and secure atmosphere, along with the development of support resources specifically for the end users of the programs. The practice of API management centers around the goal of making sure that the needs of various developers and applications, which make use of APIs, are constantly being met and any issues they have regarding APIs are efficiently tackled.

There are two ways of availing the benefits of API management. The first method is to purchase built-in API management software. This method does not require hiring the services of an API management specialist, but it is necessary for the user of API management software to have sufficient know-how of how to use it. The second method of accessing API management services is by hiring a third-party API management provider, such as Apihee Corp. or Mashery Inc. API management software tools and third-party service providers are important and advantageous because they automate and control the connection that exists between applications that use APIs.

Secondly, there are multiple versions and implementations of APIs and the API management software makes sure that these different versions remain consistent throughout. API software is also useful for managing and monitoring traffic from every individual application utilizing APIs. It also improves the performance of the applications using APIs by managing memory and caching software. Lastly, it prevents the misuse of APIs by securing the set of standardized requests in multiple procedures and policies.

APIs are not a new invention and have been in use for some time, but the increased developments and maturation in API software have allowed it to evolve and expand to cloud computing. Software creators can now release the platforms that they use on Clouds, coupled with their respective APIs, and then third-party developers can use the platform and customize it in whatever way they desire, accomplishing the same things as a custom software would but with half the hassle and effort. The self-service character of APIs has very aptly been termed as the 'consumerization of development'.

Cloud-based applications are a form of cloud computing, which is an internet-based computing, that allows servers from remote locations to store and then access data or computer services and resources from an online store called cloud storage. Clouds can either be open to the public, restricted to private use or a mixture of both public and private, in which not all of the data stored in the cloud is available to the public. One major advantage of the cloud computing is that the data or resources stored in the cloud can be accessed from any location and any device and the user doesn't necessarily have to be connected to the internet.

If the cloud storage is open to the public, they can also be accessed by anyone in need of the information or resources on the cloud, resulting in sufficiently maximizing the effectiveness of the shared resources. Another benefit of the cloud storage is that it does not take up any storage space on the hardware device of the user. Storage for Cloud applications is also much safer as the Cloud providers make sure that the servers are equipped with useful features like disaster recovery, firewall security and backups.

Given the multiple advantages associated with cloud computing, there have been many successful attempts at enhancing the cloud experience by enabling cross-cloud compatibility, helping in forming the Cloud API environment. Cloud APIs are interfaces used to build applications in the burgeoning cloud computer market. Cloud APIs enables application and programs to request and access data from one or multiple services, whether it is through a direct or an indirect interface depends on the requirements of the user.

There are two types of Cloud APIs, vendor specific and cross-platform. Cross-platform cloud computing APIs have the plus point of allowing users to access different services from multiple providers without having to undergo the hassle of rewriting. But compared with vendor specific Cloud solutions, cross-platforms have many limitations and comparatively less functional. Cloud APIs are divided into three distinct types of APIs, namely infrastructure, service and application clusters and different applications may combine these three APIs according to the need.

Cloud-based computing has become an essential component of the operations of many organizations. APIs just makes cloud-based computed much more convenient and efficient. This is because whenever an organization wishes to hire a cloud developer, they have to employ precious resources to provide a way for the developer to customize and modify their cloud platforms to that organization's specific needs and structure. With the use of APIs, developers and organizations can avoid undergoing the tediousness and easily plug together two or more different technologies and launch services that use them swiftly.

The convenience afforded by the flexibility and adaptability of APIs has accelerated the use of cloud-based apps. This is because, with the help of APIs, every cloud application can easily be modified to the requirement of a particular organization. Furthermore, it can facilitate the interaction of one organization with another by providing these two distinct identities, a shared database, which they use for their own liking. Such an easy use of cloud computing enabled by the APIs makes it possible for companies in remote regions to expediently engage in business dealings, leading to a flourishing economy and the growth and development of many businesses.

Open311 Standard Protocols

An open standard protocol, which is used by the Open311 API, is a standard that can easily be accessed and used by the general public. It is a non-propriety protocol, which is under the control of an organization, but is open for any institution or individual who wishes to make use of it. The main purpose of this open standard protocol adopted by the Open311 API is to make government databases more accessible to the citizens, resulting in an improved integration between different cities, along with decreased levels of duplication. The main purpose behind the development of Open311 API using the open standard protocol was to provide a solution to the four main drawbacks of other similar well-intentioned applications that aimed to facilitate government interaction with its citizens.

The first big issue associated with those applications was that governments had to deal with the problem of managing and controlling many different channels of communication and applications and that proved to be an extremely time consuming and tedious task. Secondly, for some of the developed applications, many of the users were unclear, whether their service requests were being addressed or whether they were even getting through to the respective government officials? This drawback with these applications led citizens to question their effectiveness and so; not many of the people opted to use them.

Another issue that added to the ineffective nature of these applications was that several of them were not connected to the official government databases and so, the communication channels provided by these applications, basically, led to nowhere. Lastly, most of the applications were not compatible with each other, leading to the problem of there being several applications that dealt with similar civic issues. Such a plethora of available applications at their service led to many overwhelmed and confused citizens

The open standard protocol of Open311 API provides an efficient solution to the major issues outlined above. The open standard enables governments to make their databases available to the general public and the public, even with minimum instructions regarding Open311's use, can easily use the platform. Secondly, the Open311 API creates an online forum where the citizens of a city can post their ideas and suggestions and also carry out productive discussions related to different community concerns.

At the same time, the users of Open311 are assured that it is directly linked to the respective city's Customer Relationship Management (CRM) systems, providing them with the guarantee that government officials are taking note of their service requests. Furthermore, it provides the government and citizens with a unified platform where all the information from different RSS feeds and linked applications end up, saving them the confusion and hassle of managing many different applications. Overall, the open standard protocol of Open311 API excels at making government databases useful and openly available to the citizens. It is also an important evolutionary step in improving the government-to-citizen communication channels, ensuring a more efficient government and more satisfied citizens.

Open311 Cities

Since Washington D.C first implemented the open standard protocol application Open311, it has spread to various cities, mostly on the North American side. One of the newest cities to launch its own Open311 application is Chicago. Although it could've availed the services of Open311 years ago, Chicago first implemented this open standard software in October, 2012. Application developers linked Open311 to Chicago's conventional 311 databases, which had been created in 1997.

The interaction of the Open311 platform with the existing 311 databases allows for an improved and faster user experience because it enables citizens to conveniently make reports with the aid of cell phones or other devices, foregoing the hassle of making lengthy phone call attempts to the relevant authorities. Before the official launch of Open311, a survey was carried out by the employees of the organization called Code for America.

This survey was done to find out the most frequently reported community problems so that they could be integrated in the service request interface of the Open311. The survey revealed that there were 14 different types of issues that were frequently reported and required fast action by the relevant authorities.

The launch of Open311 was also a part of partially fulfilling the Chicago Forward Action Agenda. The Chicago Forward Action Agenda agreed upon partnering with a firm named 'DoIT' to find different ways that their citizens could use their smart phones, specifically the camera function of their smart phones, to augment the existing 311 system, specifically targeting the surface public transportation network. The Chicago Forward Action Agenda was the outcome of a movement called Sustainable Chicago 2015.

The Chicago Forward Action Agenda revolves around Chicago's transportation sector. It promises to develop a surface transportation system that is sustainable as well as environmentally friendly, along with being a safe and enjoyable mode of transportation for the public of Chicago. The involvement of the general public, through the Open311 application, would act as a helping hand in furthering the achievement of the objectives of the Chicago Forward Action Agenda, simultaneously improving the public transportation sector of Chicago by making it safer and more accessible. It would also make Chicago's transportation sector more environmentally friendly and aid in vastly reducing the detrimental carbon emissions and carbon footprints of the cars and vans.

The emergence of the Open311 application in Chicago has allowed citizens to forego the tedious minimum six to ten minute wait that they have to endure in order to report a request and then check its status. The new process of reporting a community issue involves the citizens of Chicago simply by using one of the four applications developed by the private institutions. These four, third-party applications are SeeClickFix, ChicagoWorks, Fix311 and Georeporter.

SeeClickFIx is available on a variety of operating software, including Android, iOS and Blackberry, along with Windows. It allows citizens to upload requests, possibly with pictures, to the website where the relevant authorities then address the reported issue. To encourage participation, most of all the active members achieve rankings.

Similarly, ChicagoWorks is operating software that was created in 2011 by the 47th ward, Alderman, who when elected, wanted that service request to be submitted directly to his office. ChicagoWorks was recently updated to interact and work together with the Open311 application. But, ChicagoWorks has a shortcoming, in the sense that it does not allow users to keep track of their service requests. Fix311, on the other hand, allows users to submit service requests and enables them to keep track of them as well, ensuring that the citizens can see the progress made on their service request.

Lastly, GeoReporter is another application that allows service requests to be made and tracked and it has been expanded to include the area of Chicago since December 2012. All these third-party applications that utilize the platform of the Open311, along with many other collaborative applications that have been developed, currently entertain 14 different types of service requests. These 14 service request types can be listed as:

1. Pavement Cave-In Survey;
2. Abandoned Vehicle report;
3. Alley Light Out;

4. Sansitation Code Violation;
5. Graffiti Removal;
6. Restaurant Complaint;
7. Rodent/ Rat Complaint;
8. Building Violation Complaint;
9. Pothole in Street report;
10. Tree Debris;
11. Street Light All/ Out;
12. Street Cut Complaints;
13. Traffic Signal Complaints;
14. Street Light 1/ Out.

However, the services provided by the Open311 application still have a lot of space for the improvement in terms of reducing costs of usage, speeding up the service fulfillment process, etc. One possible suggestion given by users of Open311 is that there should be responding reports to the service requests of the citizens. Responding reports could be in the form of specifications on the website as to the nature of the work being completed, along with a feature that involves the respective workers posting pictures of the completed civic work.

Such helpful features would aid in improving the level of transparency afforded by Open311 applications and it would encourage citizens to make an increased use of its services. For the purpose of continued work on the Open311 platform, the Department of Innovation and technology has opened feedback to its users. The users can give feedback, in the form of ideas, for different types of service requests that can be added to the existing list along with suggestions that can help increase the transparency, efficiency and accountability of the governing body.

The services of Open311 are also available in a number of other cities, like Bloomington, New York City, Sans Francisco, Albuquerque, Louisville, etc. A lightweight version of Open311 was deployed in Bloomington by its Information Technology Services (ITS) department. The Open311 application that is operational in Bloomington has a companion server along with the mobile integrated applications, meaning both the server and the mobile applications are an open source and can conveniently be used by other cities and municipalities to make use of the Open311 services in their communities.

The Open311 applications of Bloomington make use of the GeoReport servers that make it easier for the authoritative organizations to keep track of all the reported public concerns and their locations.

In New York City, it was observed that the majority of the calls made to the conventional 311 centers was regarding enquiries related to questions about different city services that are available or requests for information regarding where to pay a city bill, employment opportunities, affordable housing areas, etc. All the queries had one thing in common; they revolved around the theme of social and civic services. The conventional manner in which 311 contact centers address such questions is that they re-route the phone calls to another contact center, like a 211 contact center, that deals specifically with addressing such enquiries.

The data used by both the 311 and 211 contact centers have a similar structure and can easily be covered by a standardized application programming interface (API). This observation led to the development of a novel draft standard named 'Open311 Inquiry API' by Andrew Nicklin from the New York City's Department of Information Technology and Telecommunications[18]. But as it is a recent development, the Open311 inquiry API is still a work-in-progress.

Currently, the application can only be used to access the government's database to find answers for different civic service related queries. But, the IT community is enthusiastic about the prospects of evolving Open311 Inquiry API to allow users to post answers to the questions submitted by other users. Such technological tweaks to the Open311 Inquiry API would establish it as a standard for the frequently asked questions of the traditional 311 contact centers.

Similarly, Sans Francisco's very own Open311 API, named 'SF311' also facilitates the workings of non-emergency civic services, which was the result of collaboration between developers, with the backing of nonprofit organizations and cities. The official Sans Francisco API, SF311, is currently available on Android and iPhone platforms. The third-party applications that make use of Sans Francisco's API is CitySourced, Fix311.com, SeeClickFix and SF PUC. CitySourced is an application that enables citizens to report various

---

[18]   'How Might We Improve the Way Citizens and Governments Interact?', Knight Foundation News Challenge.

public concerns, like an abandoned car or waste, to the open standard 311 platform and the SF PUC concentrated on problems related to water, power or sewer emergencies.

Efforts are being made by officials to make the SF 311 more effective by educating citizens on how to efficiently use this platform. The effectiveness of the Open311 API is swiftly becoming well known and since it is an interesting new way interacting with the official bodies of a city, it is spreading to many other cities as well. Most cities are encouraging for the further development of the third-party applications using the Open311 API, by inviting citizens and developers from any location to attempt to create a new application.

Cities, most prominently Canada, are encouraging development of the third-party applications by providing for the interested candidates and developers with the mock-up solutions which can then be used in the development and testing of their applications. Such avid interest in the Open311 API platform promises a bright future for it and the civic services that it provides.

Open311 and the Code for America

Code for America (CFA) is an organization that works on strengthening the structure of the democratic government in different cities of the America. It believes in facilitating the governing bodies to work for the people and by the people. It aims to do so by developing an open source technology through which

CFA then organizes a network for the people, who are dedicated to the purpose of facilitating government service and ensuring that it is simpler, convenient to use and more effective in addressing the various public concerns. CFA is mainly a platform through which engineers and developers connect with the government of the different cities.

After four years of work in over 32 governments of America, CFA has been able to isolate a set of important capabilities that aid cities in taking full advantage of CFA's services. The effective use of these capabilities allows cities to be more open to innovative problem-solving techniques and culture by embracing advanced tools and approaches to address community concerns. If used in the right manner, cities could also leverage technology and data to augment interaction with its citizens.

The key approaches that can be applied by cities to fully utilize the services of CFA and to foster the collaboration with its residents, can be listed as:

1. Design for the people;
2. Default to open;
3. Listen to the community;
4. Collaborate with others;
5. Leverage data for better decisions;
6. Create a greater choice of tools;
7. Organize for outcomes.

The first key capability requires government to design practices that are more human-centered. They can do so by conducting research with its citizens to get a better idea of what the resident needs, how they act and who exactly they are, as in order for a governing body to provide a more effective service, they first need to have a clearer picture of the citizens they are serving. This human-centered approach ensures an effective access to the civic services and information that are molded exactly according to the understanding and needs of the citizens.

Secondly, in order to apply the key capability of 'default to open', a government needs to make the public data freely accessible by ensuring that it is in an open and standardized format. The easy availability of the public data makes the actions of the government more transparent and accountable and also encourages increased civic engagement in the civic services.

Furthermore, when a governing body is accurately aware and concerned with the interests and opinions of the citizens that they serve, they are better able to tailor their services to efficiently cater to the real needs of their societies. In order to 'Listen to the community' governments need to create an inclusive online as well as offline channels of communication with its public and get its residents' opinions about every decision or topic that they concerns them.

After obtaining knowledge about the exact needs of its citizens, a government also needs to make sure that its public is assured that their input was an essential part of any policy-making process. By forming an open channel with its residents, a government can also tap into the skills and experiences of its residents, local institutions and community groups. By using the resources of these local institutions and organizations a government can further perfect its provision of civic services. The government can also facilitate and enable the community, improving efforts and innovations of the local institutions and organizations, ultimately resulting in the betterment of their own city.

One of the most widely known ventures of Code for America is the promotion of the Open311 API. Code for America is also responsible for bringing the services of the Open311 API to the city of Chicago. The city of Bloomington was also a finalist in competing for a contract with Code in America for its services, but in the end, Chicago was chosen. The government of Chicago felt that through the use of the traditional 311 contact center system for submitting service request reports, many citizens felt that their requests were not being heard.

So, in 2012, Chicago joined hands in collaboration with Code for America for the purpose of the deployment of the renowned open standard Open311 API. Chicago believed that the launch of Open311 API would get them access to a plethora of applications that use the web and mobile interfaces, ultimately revolutionizing the channel that the citizens of Chicago used to convey service requests to the authorities.

With the help of CFA, Chicago's technical authorities conducted interviews with more than 70 city partners, leaders and educators, along with an overview of the city's existing database of service requests, CFA was able to get an informative insight into the existing 311 process and how to improve it. This research led to the development of various services including 3111. fm, a framework for a map-based daily service tool and a tracker application named Service Tracker.

Other impressive projects that resulted from the collaboration of CFA and the Smart Chicago Collaborative, include names such as 311Labs, The Daily Brief, Open311 Status, Civiz and Civics Garden. 311Labs is a platform where different developers with ideas regarding the Open311 API could get together and provide their input. The daily Brief is an application which allows a user to filter service requests by any specific requirement relating to the location, status of the request and service name.

Open311 Status is a website that informs users about the working status of the Open311 API and whether the application is experiencing any performance issues, etc. Civics Garden is an application that records and reminds users of their civic duties and contributions and similarly, Civiz is also a civic service application. Impressed by the huge improvements in civic services brought about by the implementation of Open311 API, many other cities, like the city of Pittsburgh, are also vying for the services of CFA in order to bring the Open311 API to their cities as well.

Open 3-1-1 Projects

As we have discussed above, The Code for America is a dedicated public service organization that believes in empowering citizens and making government services easy to access and more effective. The organization encourages citizens to actively participate in their community and contribute for the greater good of the city. The organization facilitates collaborations with different local government staff members to build a problem-solving strategy through technology. The organization also provides substantial support for entrepreneurs and small start-up firms. Below, we will discuss the major 3-1-1 projects developed by The Code for America.

Open311 Dashboard

The need for an open311 dashboard developed when the upper management of The Code for America decided to bring a clean, visual and interactive dashboard for the citizens. The dashboard was designed using the Django program and Geospatial database. According to The Code for America, the open311 dashboard will allow citizens to monitor trends around their neighborhood along with various other community activities.

Joget open311 center

The Joget open311 center is another development of the web engineers at The Code for America. The purpose of the Joget open311 center is to help cities analyze the requests placed in the 3-1-1 call center in real-time.

Developer Libraries for 3-1-1

Open311 developer libraries are a resourceful application for the web developers who create open311 apps. Most open311 developer libraries are built with PHP and Python libraries that allow the web developers to successfully utilize the API. The PHP developer library is currently being used to create an updated Facebook application for open311.

The Code for America is always involved with technological developments that can help the community in a positive way. The organization has its own community of government officials and citizens that collaborate and learn to improve the city services. The Code for America also plays an important role in educating citizens and civic-minded individual by bringing them together through different seminars and educational workshops.

The most common seminar held at the Code for America is the annual summit that brings government officials, technologists, community members, entrepreneurs and other civic-minded individual together for three days. The individuals interact and share ideas in the three day summit to improve the city system efficiencies. In the past, the Code for America has developed various projects for open311 that have positively contributed towards bringing the local government departments and community members closer. Today, the organization continues to support an improved technology for the betterment of the citizens.

If we look at both the public service entities closely (3-1-1 and the Code for America), we can see a lot of similarities; both the entities are working towards achieving a harmonized community for a greater growth and development. The Code for America works in close association with the open311 to provide improved services to the citizens.

The organization sees 3-1-1 service as a communication channel that connects citizens with the various public service departments. The open311 was created to standardize the 3-1-1 project so that citizens can access the 3-1-1 anywhere. Apart from the above-mentioned projects, The Code for America uses various open311 apps for the community development and communication.

CHAPTER 5

Developments in Non-Emergency Services

Latest Developments in Open311 System

The increasing implementation of the Open311 system all over except in some American cities has led to vast improvements in the civic service delivery and government transparency. But there are still many bugs and issues that need to be worked out in the system in order to make Open311 more accessible and efficient, as with any novel technology there is always a room for improvement. Apart from the need for an improvement, such interactive technologies also require frequent updates to keep up with the fast-paced, progressive world around us.

The open standard protocol of the Open311 system has also been extremely helpful, as it allows any new developers to work with the standardized system and create a new third-party applications that further enhances an efficient delivery of a non-emergency civic services. As the population of the cities expand at an increasing rate, giving birth to a myriad of old and new community issues, such developments in applications like Open311 become even more critical, ensuring harmony among societies, while also being important for strengthening the relationship between a government and its electing citizens.

One such helpful development was brought about by a political worker of the Alderman office in Chicago, Illinois. The Alderman office collaborated with a web and mobile development organization named 2Pens Media and came up with an Open311 application called ChicagoWorks. ChicagoWorks is only supported by the iPhone iOS at the moment, but its developers are working on making it compatible with the Android operating system as well. This application facilitates the service request process by allowing users to use their phone cameras and take videos and pictures of any community issues that requires attention. These photographic service requests are then sent to the Alderman office via email along with the GPS coordinates of the location of the public concern. Such an application development would not have been possible without the open standard protocol of the Open311 API, which enabled an independent software development firm like 2Pens Media to access Chicago's data infrastructure and use it to create ChicagoWorks.

The original version of the ChicagoWorks application did not perform the function of feeding requests directly into the Chicago 311 government system, but a recent update allows the application to do just that. There is still one drawback to this application's ability to collaborate with the current 311 system, as the images sent through ChicagoWorks cannot be delivered directly to Chicago's current 311 system.

This is because the current 311 system cannot support receiving photographic images and videos, but the ChicagoWorks application works around this issue by first emailing the service requests along with the images to the ward office, which will then independently forward the requests to the respective city departments.

This updated version of the ChicagoWorks application improves the service request process in four simple steps. Firstly, when the application is used, it recognizes the ward that the user is from. It then enables the user to make a service request which goes directly to the 311 system of the city. The Alderman office in that area will then receive the user's request and the tracking number. Once a user's service request has been successfully submitted, the user receives a tracking number from the application, allowing the individual to conveniently monitor and track the progress being made on their service request.

Another city that has successfully implemented the Open311 API is Sans Antonio. This led to the city of Sans Antonio being recognized as one of the 2013-2015's top 13 citizen engaged cities in America. This prestigious designation was given to Sans Antonio by the Public Technology Institute of the National League of Cities, which is primarily a nonprofit technology institute. The Public Technology Institute applauds Sans Antonio for its achievement of the best practices for the use of 311 services and internet and mobile technologies aimed at improving the communication infrastructure of the city. These best practices implemented by the Sans Antonio included an augmented citizen participation process, the development of integrated communication channels and improved technology for the reporting of performance measures. Due to the successful implementation and encouraging results of the Open311 API, Sans Antonio has been working on further developing it.

One recent development of the application is of a 311 mobile application which is available for both Apple and Android mobile devices. The 311 mobile application allows residents to put forward their service requests directly to the city of Sans Antonio. These service requests cover a variety of issues such as overgrown yards, aggressive and dangerous animals, roadkill, graffiti, etc. The citizens can also utilize a 311 online self-service portal. Furthermore, residents can also make use of various online resources that are currently available, when seeking the city services. These services are accessible at any time of the day or night and can easily be found at www.Sansantonio.gov.

To further improve the services of its Open311 API, the City of Sans Antonio has also developed a graphical representation that displays all the service requests generated by the citizens through 311, online self-service portals and any services being delivered by the City staff. This graphical representation allows citizens to view the locations of all the city services being provided in their neighborhoods and throughout the city. The updated Open311 system gives details regarding the type of service request, the location of the request, the status of work being done and the tentative timeline in which the service request will be carried out. The Open311 system provides citizens with the latest information about the city issues and events, as it is updated on an hourly basis and it is also capable of storing case-specific information for up to seven days. This ensures that citizens are fully informed at all times about the civic services being provided by the government and validates the efficiency and effectiveness of the governing body.

Another big advancement in the Open311 API centers around the fact that a majority of the calls at the traditional 311 contact centers revolved around various queries about different government services; in other words, citizens didn't just call in to request a non-emergency civic service, but they also called in to make requests for information regarding non-emergency civic services. For example, the 311 service centers in Philadelphia recorded on average over 70 percent calls that were made by citizens, not to request services, but to ask questions related to the provision of civic services. This led to the recent development of an open standard that could be used to answer inquiries about the government services, called 311 Inquiry API.

The first version of the 311 Inquiry API was developed in early 2014 by the government of New York City in collaboration with an information technology organization. The 311 Inquiry application allows users access to the city's information database and enables them to retract information regarding the different services and facilities provided by the government, along with a comprehensive list of frequently asked questions. The 311 Inquiry application also provides a constantly updated RSS live feed, which keeps updating users about the different civic service related issues and the work being done on them.

There are two distinct functionalities for each separate function provided by the 311 Inquiry API. The first important function of the application is the 'Get Service' functionality. The Get Services functionality can be used through two methods. The first method is the 'Get Service List' function which retrieves a list of all the different services provided by the government. It gets the links to all the services along with a concise description of each service as well. The user can further restrict the list of services returned for a query by mentioning the specific category of the services they are looking for. By providing a service category, the users will be able to access a service list that only mentions the different services that come under the mentioned category.

The second method of using the 311 Inquiry API is the 'Get Service' function. When the Get Service command is used, the application retrieves elaborate information regarding the service requested. By using this function, the citizens can satisfy their curiosity related to any of the different civic services provided by their government and in turn it makes them more active in their communities.

Secondly, the 311 Inquiry API provides citizens with access to information regarding the range of facilities that are available in a city. Facilities are defined as recreational activities provided by the city government. The Get Facility function of the 311

Inquiry API works in a way similar to the Get Service functionality. The Get Facility List command provides the user with a list of links with descriptions of all the facilities that are available within the city limits. The information retrieved can also be restricted according to a specified category. The Get Facility function allows users' access to the details of any one facility that they specify. The 311 Inquiry API is also able to access the city's database of Frequently Asked Questions (FAQs). The FAQs are those questions that are most often directed at the conventional 311 contact centers and have maintained in the form of a database by the government.

The first method of using this function is the Get Frequently Asked Questions List command which retrieves a list of FAQs along with their answers. This method also allows the users to restrict the FAQs list according to a specific category. The Get Frequently Asked Questions command retrieves the specified FAQ and the relevant answer. Lastly, the 311 Today feature of the 311 Inquiry API keeps users updated by providing them regular daily status messages, giving them information on the Public Schools, Recycling pick up spots, etc. The 311 Today feed also provides announcement about any major current events that are happening in the city. Fundamentally, the 311 Today function is an RSS feed which keeps users constantly updated about the different services and activities being carried out in the city. The 311 Today feed consists a total of 39 days of 311 Today data, covering the current day along with the information about the past seven days and the future 31 days.

Further work is being carried out on improving the 311 Inquiry API and the development of the 311 Inquiry API version two.

While the 311 Inquiry application is very helpful for citizens, it is even more essential for the governments and municipalities. This is because there are huge real costs associated with the amount of calls that are made to 311 contact centers. A report by the Pew Charitable Trust carried out a review of the budget allocations made by the government to 311 contact centers, along with the amount of calls that the call centers in 15 large American cities received. The report found that the average cost per call was around 3.39 dollars[19]. That would be a staggering amount if paired with the number of calls that the 311 contact centers receive.

This fact further necessitates the development of different applications based on the 311 Inquiry API, as with the help of 311 Inquiry API, the governments of cities can lower the volume of telephone calls that are made to 311 contact centers and hence, drive down the costs associated with the operation of these 311 contact centers. Not only would these self-service applications built on the 311 Inquiry API reduce the costs linked with the amount of 311 calls, they would also assist the government in ensuring a better allocation of their existing city resources.

---

[19]   'The Next Big Thing: Open311 Inquiry API', Civic Innovations.

Improvements in the 311 Inquiry API would lead to a better allocation of municipal resources in a very important manner. There will always be individuals who are not able to self-serve due to their lack of access to the internet, any sort of mobile device or simply because they do not know how to handle technology. These people have no alternative to making a call to the local 311 contact centers. But there are other individuals who have no trouble using self-serving devices and services, for example, there are people who are extremely tech-savvy or have access to the web and mobile devices. The individuals who do not know how to gain access to self-serving methods of civic service are more efficiently handled by the 311 contact center workers and so the availability of self-serving applications like 311 Inquiry API allow the expensive and valuable resources of traditional 311 contact centers to be specifically allocated to the citizens who need it the most.

Another improvement made on the Open311 API was by The Code for America's fellow Michael Evans, brought about in 2011. In order to enhance the functions of the Open311 API, Michael Evans undertook and successfully completed a project to make creative visualizations for the system. The result of the project was the development of the Open311 Dashboard. The Open311 Dashboard aims to find a more easily understandable and presentable way in which the flood of information can be displayed. So it translates all the Open311 data into an interactive dashboard through which citizens can get an idea of the service request response times. The citizens will also be able to identify various 311 trends and patterns in a city and across the country.

The Open311 Dashboard not only helps the citizens of a country, but it also assists the city administrators by providing them with the data regarding the efficiency of the different city services. When the city administrators are more aware about the effectiveness of their services, they will be able to improve on the ones that are not efficient, resulting in the government building a better relationship with their citizens. The Open311 API allows users to view how responsive the city authorities have been in responding to the service requests on a week-to-week basis. It also has functions that allow users to zoom into specific neighborhoods or even individual city blocks. Ongoing efforts are being made to evolve Open311 Dashboard into a block-based heat map that points out where certain request types are mostly made or in what areas the government takes the time to respond to a service request.

An important name that cannot be overlooked when discussing the emergence and development of the open standard protocol Open311 is the CitySDK which stands for a City Service Development Kit. CitySDK is a development kit that is available for cities and various developers who wish to make use of the harmonizing APIs. The APIs available with CitySDK enable the development of many new services and applications by providing an assortment of tools and information that can be used by both, the government of different cities and the developers interested in APIs. The purpose of the tool kits developed and supported by

CitySDK is to encourage citizen participation in non-emergency civic services and to increase the mobility of applications aimed at facilitating the provision of the civic services. The Open311 API is also one of the components provided by CitySDK.

One of the main aims of the CitySDK is to make city resources and databases more freely available by making them accessible online, which is achieved through the development of systems like Open311 API, Tourism API, Linked Data API and Discovery Service. Discovery Service is a CitySDK component that allows users to swiftly find out which cities and databases are supported by CitySDK. Whereas, Linked Data API focuses on increasing the mobility of various databases by working within the Open Street Map application to provide a mapping interface. Lastly, the Tourism API was created so that tourists could conveniently identify different tourist spots and city events that might interest them in a particular city. Furthermore, CitySDK hopes to make the APIs more reliable and it achieves this by carrying out rigorous tests and making the applications go through a number of quality control processes. Lastly, CitySDK wants that the development and evolution of APIs and city service tool kits enable a more sustainable future for different communities.

The development of an updated version of the GeoReport API is also expected. The GeoReport API allowed developers to create applications that could both view and report issues which the authorities in a government are responsible for addressing, along with the location of each report or service request.

It is mainly designed to enable governments and developers to come up with a new applications and technologies that can easily integrate and work by using the resources of the conventional official contact centers that support the open standard protocol.

Developers have been able to come up with a second version of GeoReport which enables the report of location-based non-emergency issues in different communities, like broken street lights, stray animals, and so on. To encourage further development of systems like the Open311 API, many different governments have put into process competitions and initiative to come up with improvements on the existing Open311 API or to come up with different applications that run on the Open311 API.

Chicago is one such example of governments trying to foster the evolution of Open311 APIs. Mayor Emanuel gave the call for the next phase of the Open311 API in August 2014 by launching an extremely comprehensive public engagement strategy aimed at increasing the involvement of the residents of Chicago in the development of improved 311 systems. There is a reason for such a profound focus on the improvement of the Open311 API and that is such API systems are the future or civic services and civic engagement and without them, it is impossible to make any significant progress in the field of civic services.

CHAPTER 6

Open311 Applications

TweetMy311

TweetMy311 was an application launched in the city of Sans Francisco that enabled citizens to connect to the Open311 network with the help of their twitter accounts. TweetMy311 ran with the tagline "Better Cities, one tweet at a time." The service allowed users to report and make requests regarding non-emergency situations by using the online social networking service, Twitter. The citizens using the TweetMy311 application were able to create new requests and could make queries about the status of existing requests. The use of hash tags and geotagging automatically directs the tweets to the concerned departments.

Mark Headd was the developer of the TweetMy311 application; he states that he was always interested in building the application, however, most 311 systems had not been deployed to the Open311 API and as soon as Sans Francisco introduced the API system, Mark initiated the work on the application. The application was launched in May 2010. Let us view some of the 140 character non-emergency request made through the TweetMy311 application.

Tweet#1
"Mark Headd @mheadd 11 May 2010@tweetmy311 Public sign spray painted. #graffitisign http://twitpic.com/1hinga"

In response to the tweet regarding the issue of a public sign being painted, the TweetMy311 registers a report to the Open311 system and forwards the reference ID of the complaint to the user. Reply:
"@mheadd Request successfully submitted. Service request ID: 295842. The City's goal to have the sign fully fu... [more] http://cli.gs/d7Xpz"

A user who had registered a report to the Open311 system through TweetMy311 application wants to inquire about the status of his request and does so with another tweet.

Tweet#2
"@tweetmy311 #status 295841"

TweetMy311 checks up with the Open311 system and immediately sends a response in the following tweet.
"@mheadd Current status of request 295841: OPEN"

One of the most prominent services offered by TweetMy311 was to use the function of Mark-a-spot through tweet311. Mark-a-spot is a fully responsive mobile and desktop tool to address public civic issue. Hashtags in the tweets such as #graffitisign and

#status make the organization of data and requests extremely simple and ensure smooth flow of requests. There were three simple prerequisites for the user to make use of the service. Firstly, the person needs to own a smartphone with GPS and a camera; the user also needs to have an account on Twitter. You should be able to practice geotagging using your twitter account. In addition, to use the Mark-a-spot services the tweet must have two characteristics, the longitude and latitude of the location that the user is tweeting from and also a valid hashtag that maps to the specific service type that the user wants to employ. TweetMy311 also started operations in Washington DC but aborted the overall operations in July 2011. Many other such applications, which had taken inspiration from the TweetMy311 project, were launched such as CitySourced.

A twitter user who used the application tweeted:

"@mattjfriend 16 Aug 2010 Interesting and useful concept: "TweetMy311 makes it easy to submit 311 service requests using a smartphone and Twit...http://tweetmy311.org/".

HeyGov!

The HeyGov! The application was launched in April of the year 2010 and is primarily a Web 2.0 application. Web 2.0 uses improved technology rather than the static display of the early World Wide Web sites and Web 2.0 applications allow users to interact and communicate using the social media tools that are already available. In case of HeyGov! The social networking site being employed was twitter. The HeyGov! application basically provides a channel of communication for the government and the citizens. It can be used as a communication channel for any government department which entertains direct requests from the public. If the government department has an already existing customer relationship management system, the HeyGov! The app can be integrated with the CRM system of the said department.

The HeyGov! app, just like the TweetMy311 application, was first launched in the city by Sans Francisco. As the city had the Open311 system in place, HeyGov! users could use the application to make service requests for Open311 operations.

HeyGov! is extremely efficient as it uses Microsoft's cloud platform Azure. Azure provides a wide array of services such as computing, storage, networking, data collection and applications. So Azure allows HeyGov! to retrieve data from the Open311 system and moreover, it allows the data bases of both applications to be integrated.

Other than making requests for Open311 services, the HeyGov! application offers two added features that are generic map and code enforcement modules. The code enforcement module allows citizens to report desecrations concerning the local code. On the other hand the, generic map module allows the citizens to view school zones, construction zones and other similar data sets. Code enforcement violations basically include sub-standard conditions, for example inoperable doors and windows, improper garbage disposal, uncovered gutters and gullies, blocked sewage pipes and holes. This may also include flooded basements and driveways being covered by snow.

The most unique feature of the HeyGov! application is its interactive mapping application that enabled users to track and examine their reports on Open311 regarding non-emergency situations. The HeyGov! application is connected to Google maps and Bing maps as well. Let us review an example to understand the operation of the HeyGov! app.

Ms. Savannah sees an open pothole on a street while she was on her way to the local market, which could pose a potential threat to a passerby; the most important thing is to remember the location of the street with the open pothole. Next, using the HeyGov! app, mark the exact location of the area on the support maps. The information will then be forwarded to the local government so they can take action regarding the issue. The users can also track the progress of their requests and can receive latest updates on their report via email and Twitter alerts. Government departments and officials can also subscribe to the HeyGov! app to examine the requests directed to them and they can directly interact with the citizens of their community.

CitySourced

CitySourced is an organization which aims at improving real time civic engagement through mobile devices. It is an organization which works to provide citizens with simple and effective platforms empowering them to play a significant part in identifying and reporting civic issues. After being selected as a finalist in 2009 at the TechCrunch50 conference, the CitySourced application was integrated with Sans Francisco's Open311 API. CitySourced integration with the Open311 API allows the application to send reports concerning civic issues directly to Sans Francisco's 311 system, giving citizens a direct link to the city's non-emergency government offices.

CitySourced was an important advancement as it allows residents of a city to use their smartphones and devices to take photographs of important community concerns and report them, while also getting notified when the issue they reported is resolved. Furthermore, it also provides details regarding the location of the issue reported in the form of GPS coordinates, the time that the report was submitted and the category in which the report would fall.

The main purpose that the application CitySourced hopes to achieve is to make civic engagement and the provision of civic services more cost effective and efficient. It drives down costs by reducing the amount of calls that are made to the traditional 311 contact centers. It makes the provision of civic services in an efficient process by providing a direct and open channel of communication between the government of the city and its residents. It also makes managing a diverse set of data a less daunting task for city employees.

In Sans Francisco, CitySourced was initially only available on the Apple iOS but around 2010 it was launched on the Blackberry and Android platforms as well, making the application more accessible for users. CitySourced is available in over 1900 cities all over America, including Sans Jose and Los Angles, and is powered by one of the largest databases of the public officials in America, named FreedonSpeaks. CitySourced provides governments with the technology to use money more efficiently and makes them more accountable to the citizens that they govern; at the same time it encourages citizens to participate in civic services and make their own communities a better place to live.

The CitySourced application has a very user friendly interface and the process of using it is very simple. To report a problem, a user has to download the CitySourced application to their phone and load it. Once it is open they have to select the category in which they issue them are reporting falls into, for example the user has to choose whether it is a trash issue or a pothole issue. In the next step the user has to supply a brief description of the issue under consideration. After taking a photograph to complement the description of the civic issue, the user just has to upload the report to the prominent social platform of Twitter. The uploaded information contains the GPS coordinates of where the user is reporting from. The application then routes the tweet or reports directly to the concerned city hall or authorities.

MojiPge

Another similar interactive and helpful mobile application is the Moji Page application developed by the Moji Labs, Inc. Moji Page is a very customizable application that is also free of cost. It is an extremely convenient platform for access to different categories of information in a summarized and accessible interface. It gives users a link to their most used web content, such as social networks and live news feeds. It summarizes all the information in a single screen in the form of different widgets that connect users to the content of their choice. Moji page can be termed as the Google search engine for mobile devices. Moji Page works on both mobile phones and computer desktops.

The distinctive feature of Moji page is that it is especially streamlined to enhance the mobile experience, as the developers of this application designed it while keeping in mind the specific limitations of mobile devices. So all the content on Moji Page is organized in a way that specifically optimizes it for viewing and browsing on mobile devices. This application is also easily accessible because it can be customized and personalized to be set up as the default home page on the user's mobile browser. Moji Page is also designed to be compatible with any web browser that is available on the user's mobile device or desktop. It also provides users with a faster browsing experience because the content available on this application does not redirect the users to another website that takes time to load. Lastly, Moji Page is also extremely cost effective as it is free of charges and incurs the minimum amount of mobile data usage costs because it restricts the download of unwanted content.

Moji Page is an open standard system which allows various developers to create content by using simple application programming interfaces (APIs). The open API format of Moji Page enables developers to come up with their own widgets, which are then made available on the Moji Page application. In order to ensure a consistent user experience, Moji Labs, Inc. also provide developers with technical support and documentation to make sure that the widgets they create work in the same format. Unlike other conventional mobile pages, the technology behind Moji page enables content to be loaded directly from the server instead of the browser, allowing the Moji Page application to be compatible with the largest variety of mobile devices available. Moji Page has also created a widget for Open311 which opens up a new dimension of civic engagement for users. The Open311 widget allows residents to select widgets that they want to use. Each of the widgets can work within any city because they are backed by a standard government API.

Service Tracker

Another Open311 API friendly application that augments the civic service delivery process is Chicago's Service Tracker. Service Tracker was created by the nonprofit organization named Code for America. It is a website that is compatible with mobile browsing as well, and allows its users to update themselves about the status of their 311 calls. After submitting reports regarding various civic issues, the residents of Chicago can also track the progress that has been made on their service requests, in the same way that an individual tracks the location of a package on its way through a delivery service. When a user submits a service report, they are provided with a tracking number. The user can then enter the tracking number into the Service Tracker website and get information on whether their request has been completed or is under progress. The website also informs the user about what city is handling the service request. Furthermore, the website provides the user with a list of recent service requests along with the details about when and where the various requests were submitted.

Residents and developers of the Service Tracker website hope that it will play a part in making the government of Chicago's actions more transparent and accountable to the general public. Increased accountability and transparency was also one of the objectives that Mayor Rahm Emanuel hoped to achieve during his term in office. However, despite the innovative nature of the Service Tracker website, there are still some problems and limitations. The Service Tracker provides no option for a user to search the 311 database by address or location. In order to find the address or location specific information an individual would have to use the more complicated interface of the respective city's data portal.

A casual user of the Service Tracker website will not go through the hassle of doing, so they would forego the option of reporting a service issue. Another function that the Service Tracker website does not perform is that an individual cannot report a service issue through a text message; instead, they have to send a text message to Chicago's 311 departments asking for contact information regarding the location of their area's Alderman Office. But developers are working on making such an option available to the residents of Chicago. Another limitation of the Service Tracker website is that it does not have a city-sponsored mobile application. The reason for this is that the government of Chicago believes that the third-party developers are better equipped to create a better and cheaper mobile applications than the city itself.

A collaborative application, without which the use of Service Tracker would not be possible, is the Chicago Works application. Chicago Works is a mobile application that is free of cost and allows an individual to submit a service request after which the application provides the user with a tracking number. The individual can then use the tracking number to utilize the services of the Service Tracker application and view the status of their service request. Both the Chicago Works mobile application and the Service Tracker website are based on the Open311 open standard protocol, which allows users to access the huge city database regarding 311 services. The availability of such platforms has reduced the number of calls to the 311 contact centers, making it easier to manage the work, and it has increased the number of civic service requests being made to the government, promising an upward trend in civic engagement.

The Daily Brief

The Daily Brief, currently available on the Android and Apple platform, is an application that compiles enormous amount of data from various sources, online and presents an extremely informational unified report. The Daily Brief was developed by the fellows of the renowned nonprofit information technology centered organization called Code for America. It is like an everyday newspaper, but in a summarized and concise form. The Daily Brief updates to keep the user daily, up to speed with everyday events and important news.

The Daily Brief application covers a wide array of topics such as information about local weather, airport and flight delay status, everyday headline news, the location of the cheapest local gas stations, local traffic and customized daily stock reports. It is also convenient to use as compared to other news and information applications because it does not allow random advertisements. Furthermore, the Daily Brief provides users with enhanced visuals and a user-friendly interface that makes it one of the easiest applications to use. It also provides individuals with a voice recognition feature, making it convenient and compatible for people with visual disabilities.

The new updated version of the Daily Brief that is expected to be released soon will include reports on seismic activity, amber alerts, NFL, NBA, MLS headlines and a Word of The Day feature. Also, a Daily Brief version that is compatible with the Open311 API allows users to explore and discover various service requests with a filter on neighborhood, report status and service name. The application makes use of a city's Open311 database and provides users with a picture of the real-time city service requests being reported and addressed. Another application which makes use of the Daily Brief interface and format is called Circa. Circa is an Android and Apple news reader application that displays important news by breaking it down into an easy-to-read bite-sized format.

311 Labs

311 Labs are another Code for America project. The Code for America fellows collaborate with various organizations, communities, developers and city partners to work on a wide variety of projects, which are aimed at the improvement of the civic service delivery of a government. The fellows at Code for America develop a range of applications for various purposes, be it a whimsical or serious profit-making application. One gradual emerging standard that is used by Code for America is Open311, which is an application programming interface (API) used for developing applications that make civic data present in a city's 311 system, available to the residents of that city.

Many different developers in various cities tried to make applications using the API features, which resulted in the rise of inconsistent applications that were sloppily modified to customize them to a city's own unique requirements. In order to erase such inconsistencies, the fellows at Code for America realized the need for a platform where the interested cities and organizations could experiment with the open standard API and communicate with each other. So, they developed 311 Labs, which has proven to be a vital participant in improving the provision of civic service while also encouraging civic participation among the residents.

311 Labs are a team of experts that specializes in technological innovation. These experts are able to provide their qualified services to the various organizations and cities that are interested in the development of innovative solutions regarding civic services. 311 Labs aim to act as a vessel for bringing innovative concepts to the market by gathering talent to form a cohesive team of experts. The services of 311 Labs also reduce the risks associated with the various stages of product development by using various components of proven technologies. The main focus of this team of experts is to accelerate the development of mobile and cloud based innovations along with sales management of these solutions.

The collaboration of 311 Labs and other organizations and cities has led to the launch of two innovative applications, namely the Daily Brief and Open311 Status. The Daily Brief application is already running using the Open311 APi and is available in Baltimore, Boston and Bloomington. Even though 311 Labs has only recently begun operation, it has already attracted the approval of, and feedback from, city officials and residents. But the 311 Labs team recognizes the effort of its city partners as essential to their success.

Other Platforms

As discussed in the above section, the open311 technology allows citizens to easily access the public service sites and add comments or feedback regarding a service. Most of the web platforms for the open311 are developed by renowned technology companies including Motorola, Oracle and Lagan technologies.

Before the emergence of technologically advanced open311 applications, many developers designed API integrated applications for open311 that were never consistent with the system. But today the situation is the other way round. These platforms play an important role in the public service development, which is why the major technology firms are providing improved platforms to handle the complex citizen data. For example, consider the Oracle's CX, a platform that allows 3-1-1 call centers to perform better and faster; the CX application makes it easier for the 3-1-1 call center representatives to track and monitor data to provide timely solution for various non-emergency situations. This was not possible before the emergence of advanced technological enterprise solutions.

We have already discussed some of the most common open311 applications such as Tweetmy311, HeyGov! City Sourced, 311.fm, Service tracker, the Daily Brief and 311 labs. In this section we will look at some other application or platforms, including open311 Status, Civiz, uReport, SeeClickFix and Civics Garden that are used for 3-1-1 services.

Open311 Status

There are various other platforms that make use of the Open311 API, most of which would not have been possible without the work of the Code for America fellows. Another such platform is called the Open311 Status. It is a web based platform for open311 services that allows the citizens or users to see the performance of open311 API's. Let's quickly go through the definition of API to refresh our memory. An API, application programming interface, is a set of protocols or tools that are utilized to develop open311 applications. The open311 Status lets users know about the technical issues with the API's. The platform provides citizens with API uptime citizen utilization and comprehensiveness. If the open311 API's are down or malfunctioning due to some reason, the site immediately lets the citizens know to avoid any inconvenience.

Moreover, the Open311 Status is an application that constantly monitors the performance of the Open311 APIs to see whether any of the APIs are facing performance issues or any downtime. It also provides a comprehensive set of statistics about the uptime, downtime and citizen utilization of Open311 endpoints. It helps users of Open311 APIs by providing them with information about when to use the Open311 API and when they will not get a response from the platform.

Civics Garden

Similarly, Civics Garden is another such platform that facilitates the process of civic engagement. Civics Garden is kind of a digitized, online journal which allows its users to record their civic activities. Civics Garden can also be used to set reminders for civic activities along with writing thoughts and details about a particular civic activity. It promises users that through the use of this platform, they will be able to enhance their civic life.

SeeClickFix

SeeClickFix is another web tool that enables the residents of a city to submit service requests and reports about non-emergency community issues, as a form of community engagement. The service requests generated by SeeClickFi are then communicated directly to the concerned local government. The SeeClickFix application is a web-based map that shows highlighted comments by different users. It is an open and interactive platform that can be used by any individual. People can also avail the service of email alerts about various community related topics. This tool is compatible with Apple and Android operating software. Another useful tool is the 311 FM, which is available in the city of Chicago and can be used to track, observe, analyze and compare various 311 service requests across Chicago.

Civiz

Civiz is a polygot open311 platform that operates as a service civic application. For those who are not aware, an application written in polygot programming incorporates several programming languages that perform similar operations. This platform, unlike the other open311 platform allows users to take part in a civic community that promotes city growth through civics. The platform offers civic-minded individuals a community in which they learn and participate to contribute towards their cities.

uReport

uReport is a standalone, small scale CRM or Constituent Relationship Management application that has an integrated open311 API (GeoReport v2). The uReport web application is not as commonly used as the other platforms like HeyGov, the Daily Brief and Service Tracker. The uReport application consists of context-switched feeds such as JSON AND XML. These feeds allow the application to be easily integrated into different environments.

Use of Web Applications

The use of open311 web applications can be seen in various cities that have implemented 3-1-1 call centers for the non-emergency services. For example, after the 3-1-1 service was launched in the city of Chicago, the city officials immediately introduced the Chicago's public Open311 web application. The application allowed users to have a quick access to the system and report any suspicious activity or request any information regarding the city departments. Through the open311 application, citizens can easily make quick reports online with the help of their smart phones. The application eliminates the lengthy process of placing a call to 3-1-1.

As discussed earlier, the open311 applications use Lagan technologies that also provide the CRM (citizen relationship management software) to the 3-1-1 call centers. Quite recently, the Lagan technologies, announced that their CRM software will now come integrated with open311 API. This will significantly increase the system efficiency as the 3-1-1 representatives and the agents will now be able to access citizen inquiries easily.

The open311 API is increasingly becoming popular; it is being adopted by various technology firms like Microsoft, Oracle, Lagan technologies and Motorola provide improved open311 applications. For example, the Code for America has developed various projects that integrate open311 API. The open311 API promotes collaboration, learning and openness, which was never possible before. With open311 integrated API devices, citizens can access the 3-1-1 system without any hassle. In addition, the city officials can immediately become aware of various city problems and find a timely solution.

CHAPTER 7

Free third party Apps

SeeClickFix

The introduction of Open311 to Application programming interface opened up a new era of development and many smartphone applications, in regards to the Open311, started to surface. The most significant development came when application developers were able to integrate databases and made the interaction with Open311 databases a possibility. Not only did this make the Open311 operations faster, but also increased the number of people seeking out 311 services. One of the first cities to introduce these third party applications was Chicago.

Code for America was one of the first organizations that started to develop the Open311 and initiated the collaboration. The developers at Code for America, while commenting on the Open311 system, concluded that the current Open311 system was limited and closed to a few users; however, the introduction of smartphone applications encouraged more users to make requests to the Open311 system regarding non-emergency situations.

The developers at Code for America believe that the Open311 and its application will completely transform the user's experience. With a single click, the users can take a photo of the open pothole or broken street light or any other such non-emergency site from their smartphones and map its location and that will register the report. The user can also go back and track their requests at any time and find out the status of their report.

The Open311 applications have changed the whole dynamics of the services provided by 311 non-emergency services, as they allow greater visibility for local government and municipal departments to view the requests directed their way, ensuring a more seamless process of delivering the required services.

The open standard format of Open 311 API has a number of advantages. First of all, the open API of this platform does wonders for improving service delivery. It does so through enabling third-party applications and providing a more efficient and convenient way for the visualization of data. Furthermore, it increases the level of interacting through its peer-to-peer approach focused on more efficient problem solving. The Open 311 API also enables the third party applications that use its standard, to widen their impact, reach and access new constituents.

Such smartphone friendly applications are more appealing for audiences of the younger demographic, successfully getting their interest in civic services and empowering and enabling them to work for the betterment of their societies. Furthermore, such applications using the open standard also make civic participation a more attractive activity, as these applications greatly reduce the amount of time people need to put in for a civic engagement.

With the easy accessibility guaranteed by mobile device-friendly applications, citizens can perform civic services with the easy click of a button or touch of a finger. The Open 311 API standard is also extremely helpful in facilitating efficient integration of various different systems through its internalized API, which allows for standardization over multiple systems and regions, and at the same time, ensures savings in costs and guarantees and encourages innovation through the sharing of new applications in various cities.

There are various strategies that can be used to make the implementation of Open 311 API easier. The most important strategy is regarding the development of third party applications. The open format of this platform makes it easier to share data that enable multiple third parties to develop innovative and smart applications for civic service delivery. Due to this standardized open format, anyone, a normal citizen to an aspiring entrepreneur, can take up the initiative of developing a new third-party application.

This lifts some of the responsibility of application development from the shoulders of the government and allows them to focus on other important issues. To motivate and encourage the development of such applications, many cities have given calls for competitions for the best and most innovative third party application that uses the Open 311 API, facilitating them through the application stores of different operating systems, such as Android and Apple.

This approach to the implementation of the Open 311 API is not without its challenges. The third parties that develop the application are often discouraged from such activities because of the amount of liability that falls on them, regarding any harm that is caused by the use of their third-party application that is based on the Open 311 API data. Furthermore, data are usually not a free commodity and is mostly regarded as a major source of revenue for firms. So organizations might be reluctant about the idea of giving data in return for no revenue.

However, an argument that is against this proposed statement is that the open standard API is designed for the provision of civic services and so essentially, it is paid for by the taxpayers and so it belongs to them. Furthermore, the development of any new applications that are web-based leads to problems and issues regarding digital inclusion.

This is a challenge that can be easily overcome through promoting digital literacy through civic engagement opportunities or schools and libraries. Apart from that, help can be taken from groups that specialize in digital inclusion. Lastly, there is a problem reaching the audiences who are not technology-savvy or who prefer not to use computers or web-based applications. There are quite a few out-of-date applications and technologies as well.

Service and Uses

SeeClickFix allows residents of an area or a city to report non-emergency issues and is connected to the Open311 system. The SeeClickFix has a mobile application. The SeeClickFix uses a map to mark areas and the civic issues and non-emergency sites in that area. Just like in social networking sites, the users can add comments and through these comments, the user may add additional information about a request or suggest possible solutions and also have the choice to add, upload pictures and videos.

The web tool keeps the identity of the users anonymous to encourage more users to report civic issues and at the same time, ensure transparency. The SeeClickFix website runs under the motto of "Better Communication Better Community" and believes that a communication channel between the government and the people is all that is needed to solve civic issues.

The most exclusive feature of the SeeClickFix project is its collaboration with news media. Prestigious newspapers such as The New York Times, The Philadelphia Inquirer, The Sans Francisco Chronicle, etc. are all members of the SeeClickFix project and the idea behind collaborating with the news media was to ensure accountability of the local government offices, by keeping track of their services and judging their performance with the help of the SeeClickFix service.

In addition, the news media has also been employed as a tool to increase civic participation. For instance, if any of these news media publishes an article about

SeeClickFix or its collaboration with Open311, not only will this expose the services of the application to relatively new audiences, but will also reinforce the credibility of the application which is substantial, as many people avoid using the application as they believe it is no good.

The New York Times, in an issue, printed an article concerning SeeClickFix with the title "News Sites Dabble with a Web Tool for Nudging Local Officials." In the piece, the writer discussed the function and viability of the application. The article pointed out, "apart from other hyper local sites is that, anywhere in the world, it can foster interaction among government, news media and residents."

The news piece also included the statement of Mr. Doug Hardy, the creator of the SeeClickFix web tool, who added that, "We printed a paragraph from a woman's complaint about a deteriorated mill building in Vernon," Mr. Hardy wrote in an e-mail message, "I got responses from the mayor, town administrator and the architect who is redeveloping the building — all within 24 hours.

SeeClickFix became invaluable when various city governments started using the web tool as a work order system. In the product display on the SeeClickFix website, there is an icon labeled "Mobile Applications for Officials", as evidenced by the label, the SeeClickFix service has specially designed applications and features for government officials that primarily lets officials on public office posts keep track of requests related to their departments. The main attraction that

SeeClickFix offers to government officials is that it allows them to filter requests by letting them access requests according to the specific categories they have picked out, for instance user, department and geography.

Another exclusive feature of the SeeClickFix application is that it sends out important information to users that is either city or location specific. The Geo-driven notification system allows the SeeClickFix application to mark and isolate neighborhoods for targeted alerts and notifications to the citizens of a precise locality. These notifications could contain warnings, such as storm or flood or information about the local highway being closed. These alerts could also be the updates about the events in the town such as a local spring carnival. In addition, they can also be about the city budget sessions or city council proceedings. SeeClickFix also plans to venture into natural disaster and calamity response service.

The popularity and increased usage of the SeeClickFix system can also be associated with its availability on both IOS and Android software. The tool uses Google Maps technology to help mark the locations of the registered reports. The SeeClickFix application's function is as easy as the name; it saves you from the hassle of calling and reporting and lets you detect an issue. With a single click, it enables you to capture the picture evidence of the issue and within some time, it pledges an easy fix to your problem.

The SeeClickFix applications make government workings and provision of civic services more efficient and transparent in four simple steps. In the first step, it works on improving the centralized management of different departments. This is done through the application's CRM platform which aids in managing the workflow and organization of multiple departments, mainly through making sure the service requests are routed to the correct office or department responsible for a particular area. Secondly, it also routes service requests to the respective district or county within a town or city.

Through its location-based technology, SeeClickFi makes sure that the hassle for distribution of issue requests and management of workflow is as simplified as possible. Furthermore, the application allows municipality officials to forego the hassle of using phone calls, paper and desktop computers when in the field. Instead, they can report issues and address them while they are in the field, to their respective departments, with the use of their mobile devices. Lastly, the CRM platform provided by SeeClickFix allows governments to efficiently input all their online and phone call service requests into one database, which can be easily accessed through the application. People interested in reporting civic issues can also simply attach the image of the civic issue and send it to their respective municipalities, which greatly reduces the resolution time of the issue by a huge margin.

Up till October2014, SeeClickFix has successfully addressed over a million issues and service requests. Furthermore, Detroit's department responsible for water and sewerage has also recently collaborated with the services of SeeClickFix, enabling the department to speedily respond and address the requests of Detroit's residents. Additionally, the Trentonian and the web-based SeeClickFix website has also joined together in collaboration, aiming to empower the residents of its area by giving them access to a tool that is extremely interactive and allows them to successfully report various non-emergency issues that maintain the quality of life in the area. It is extremely easy to make use of this facility, all the individual has to do is navigate and search on a map of the area where the issue that needs to be reported is located and then click on it, completing the procedure by filling out a form to which a picture can also be attached and uploaded.

Chicago Works

With the tag line of Help us Renew Chicago, the Chicago Works application allows users to make service requests that are forwarded to the Open311 system. The Chicago Works presently have more than eight thousand users.

A user of the Chicago Works application adds that he took a picture of graffiti on a public building and only three days later the graffiti was removed. He commented "It is called Chicago Works, and it does". The user also added that he never thought that something like this could be this simple and more significantly this direct in its approach.

The website of Chicago Works is as simple as the task of putting up your request or reporting a non-emergency situation. As soon as you log into the Chicago Works mobile application, there are four unique icons, each representing a diverse feature; the red star icon is where the user begins. The user needs to register all the required information such as his city, e-mail address, age, etc. After filling out the information required in the citizen information tab, the user moves on to the next step, which is to submit a request. The icon of this feature shows a blue thumbnail which is primarily an artsy representation of the key function of the Chicago Works application.

The service gives the users the option to choose from 14 different and most popular service requests. Like other applications that have been discussed earlier, Chicago Works has integrated databases with the Open311 service and as soon as a request is made, it is registered with the Open311 service. With each Open311 request a reference ID is forwarded to the user, which allows the user to track the request and enables them to find out the status of their request.

The Chicago Works application ensures transparency and accountability of public offices. Interestingly enough the Chicago Works web tool was created by Ameya Pawar. Mr. Pawar was elected to the Chicago City Council as an Alderman of the 47th Ward. The application was developed by him with the assistance of his childhood friend Dimitrios Tragas and he did so during the course of his campaign for the City Council election. As an Alderman, Ameya Pawar thought it would be used to build an application that could help him track problem or civic issues that people from the local community faced.

He stated in an interview with CBS Chicago that "I think the big deal over time as you're going to find a lot of people using this data to help inform our decisions and make government more efficient, people can see their tax dollars at work." When the Alderman, who is next to the position of Mayor of the City Of Chicago, comments on the efficacy and the standing of the Chicago works application, not only will this increase usage, it will also encourage community members to use the application as a channel of communication to get in touch with the government.

Ameya Pawar has often been described as a young, modish, hip and tech savvy guy who truly believes that using technology is the new and fresh way to address civic issues as well as increase the civic participation. The Chicago works application was developed by Ameya to interact with the members of his community and to involve community members in the resolution of problems. The Chicago Works application took its inspiration from a television show called Chicago Works that has been running in the city for the past 15 years. The award winning program would air for two hours on local television channels.

The show included feature stories highlighting the programs and initiatives of the 40+ departments and bureaus of Chicago city government, and promoted the public events that took place in the city. Chicago Works still runs a YouTube channel, which shares the same logo as the mobile phone application; the logo contains four red stars between two way blue lines, which is also the flag of Chicago city. A two-minute trailer of the City of Chicago TV, YouTube channel summarized the whole concept of Chicago Works.

In addition, it also listed the services it aimed to provide. It starts with the function of keeping the citizens of the Chicago informed about the Culture and the social events taking place in the city. This was followed by a small clip categorized City Services. The clip included video of a public official painting of graffiti on a public building wall, followed by clips of city workers removing snow from roads and picking up trash cans. The last section included agencies in the city of Chicago that are striving towards renewing Chicago, the basic aim of Chicago Works, agencies included Chicago Reads Together, Let Us Build a Better Chicago and the green project for the famous Loyal Park.

The website also has a review section that includes the experiences of the Chicago Works users. One user listed "Great Use of App Store - This is the kind of forward thinking our political leaders need to really harness the power of the App Store, and most importantly the people. It speaks volumes when we can get together and help make our city a better place. Hopefully other cities adopt this kind of community app. Also, I wanted to quickly comment on the design and how the app functions. It's very clean and simple. Can't really say anything I don't like about it. Good work from both parties involved!"

Unlike previous third party applications Chicago Works is still running strong with new and latest versions being launched every year; the latest version that is Version 2.2 was released in February 2014. There have been nine versions of the application in the market, which just goes to show how committed the developers are to give the users a valuable experience in their effort to change Chicago. The application is a real treat for the people of Chicago as it is available for free on Apple iTunes store as well as Google Play store.

Chicago Works also has a website, called Chicago Works For You, which is basically a dashboard that covers the whole city and gives a detailed view of each ward and the service delivery they are providing. On the home page of this website, a user will find a map of the whole city, which is updated on a daily basis with a summary about all the various service requests. These service requests can also be further filtered according to the ward and type of service. Furthermore, up and down-arrows are shown next to different request types showing the average amount of times that service was requested on a particular date. The higher the average of a particular service type is, the longer the up or down-arrow will be. As a default, the service type with the highest average is automatically shown as highlighted on the map.

A user can also get the detailed averages and numbers pertaining to a specific service request, on any particular day, by simply clicking on it. The website enables users to view data specific to any type of service request for any day, whether it was in the past or the present, along with allowing users to share views regarding the website on any social networking site or through email.

The service request type can be selected easily from the menu that displays the services. A user can see the weekly views of each type of service in its delivery with respect to different wards. The user can also see the details for the amount of open and closed request, with respect to each separate ward in Chicago, along with up to 500 photos of the last service requests. The City's Service Tracker's website links to Chicago Works For You's website and it is useful for viewing information about the current status and details of a particular service request.

All the data that are utilized on this website is acquired from the Open 311 API of Chicago, which allows users to both enter new service requests into the system and to view any 311 data. This data is available because of Chicago's collaborative with a nonprofit, technology-focused organization named Code for America. A team of technologists worked endlessly with the city to develop an Open 311 API for Chicago. The Service Tracker System was designed with the help of the Smart Chicago Collaborative. The Smart Chicago Collaborative is an organization that specifically works on developing technology associated with provision of civic services.

Fix311

With smartphones becoming a commonality, cities and governments are using this technological development to their advantage. One such benefit that municipalities have gained owing to smartphone technology is that they have been enabled to shift their 311 non-emergency services to Open311, which is an Application Programming Interface that has led to the development of 311 mobile applications.

Fix311 is another mobile application that takes service requests for 311 non-emergency operations. It enables the users to make use of the special features of their smartphones such as Global positioning systems and the mobile phone camera to make enhanced service requests.

For instance, if a user spots an open pothole on his/her street, open potholes are a classic example of a non-emergency situation, using your camera phone, you can take a picture of the open pothole and in addition, the GPS on your phone will mark the exact location of the open pothole. This will be of great assistance as it will give the service providers the extra information to work with.

One of the drawbacks of Open311 on Application programming interface is that if each municipality would develop their own Open311 application, the process would become extremely tedious and complicated and in addition, it would require an excessive amount of monetary investment. Therefore, the application development was left up to the third party developers and Fix311 was also developed by one such developer. However, Fix311 has also been able to overcome the shortcoming that is a mobile application scope and used to be limited to a single city.

Fix311 has the ability to connect to the Customer relationship system and is integrated with the database of Open311 in a manner where each city or municipality receives the 311 non-emergency request and these requests are forwarded from server to server to the specific Customer relationship system. Fix311 application works on the exact same structure as that of 911 emergency services, where the number remains the same in every city or municipality and despite of the same line, a system has been developed that enables a call made from a specific city to be connected to the CRM system of that very city.

The Fix311 team describes integration of the 311 system as their chief goal. It aims to make the Open311 system more centralized and make the user experience much more efficient and convenient, by giving the users the opportunity for reporting service requests from any town, municipality, district, city or state. The Fix311 operations want all concerned citizens to come on one platform so they can voice their issues on all sorts of civic issues.

Centralization of system through Fix311

What Fix311 will give you that other mobile applications of the sort do not, is that it gives the local government, municipalities and public offices the service of developing their 311 non-emergency application and it helps them bring their 311 on the API. Fix311 develops custom API and furthermore, is also able to connect it to the Customer relationship management system of the very organization.

The Fix311 offers six unique services, the foremost service is emergency management; the Fix311operations allows you to report any non-emergency situation such as a broken street light or noisy neighbors, in addition it also displays alerts to users' smartphones with the help of PUSH technology. Push technology is a form of internet or web based communication where the request for a given operation is initiated by the central server.

Fix311 assists governments and municipalities in various ways and added features of the Fix311 service which is the Smart service list enables each public office of a designated city to develop their own service list, for instance, if the 311 service in Chicago does not include tackling the issue of building violations, they can easily not include it as a service in their service list. Previously, such a difference would require a new application to be developed in the city, however, Fix311 has given the local governments an easy fix.

Features

Again the Fix311 allows you to make a civic requests and manage those requests from anywhere, as the geographical location is not a limitation in the case of the Fix311 application. The Work anywhere feature allows the users to do so with great ease.

Location awareness is probably the most useful and distinct feature of the Fix311 application; since the Fix311 application is available in multiple cities, there is a chance of confusion when it comes to the exact locality of the non-emergency situation. However, with the aid of GPS tracking and the location aware feature, Fix311 prevents its users to report from a wrong jurisdiction or locale.

The CRM and analytics feature is unique to the 311 service, the Fix311 has the special system of integrating with the organizations custom and already existent CRM system and this allows for very efficient and timely management of the civic requests for every city.

The Fix311 website, through images and screenshots, describes the convenient process of making a non-emergency request to its users. After logging into the Fix311 service, three icons will appear on the screen, namely new requests, track requests and new alerts. If you choose the first icon, the next detail you would be required to register would be to add your neighborhood. After the verification of the neighborhood, you are given a choice where you can either make the request public or private. If you choose private, your request will only be visible to the municipal authority.

However, if you choose to make your request public, it will be visible to the municipal authority as well as the general public. After this, you can add a photo of the non-emergency situation and can even add a caption to the photo. The location of the non-emergency situation is verified once more, after which the request is officially registered.

The track request icon allows you to check the progress on your request, whereas the latest alerts icon gives you the latest updates on your neighborhood, concerning civic issue as well as other city updates. The Fix311 application also provides statistical data in the form of pie charts and bar graphs, about civic problems and the response of the government to counter the problems. In this manner, local governments can also keep tabs on their performance.

GeoReporter

GeoReporter is another distinct service that allows service users to make requests to the Open311 system. GeoReporter also works in all cities and saves the local government the hassle of spending time and money to develop their own mobile application in order to connect to the Open311 server. GeoReporter is not only limited to reporting and tracking service requests, but also provides assistance to the municipalities to develop their own mobile application integrated with the Open311 system.

GeoReport V2

Another added feature of GeoReporter is the Georeport V2. The GeoReport Application programming interface v2 allows the developers to develop applications where users can both view as well as report problems concerning non-emergency situations and other civic issues, which the government and public offices are responsible for addressing. The Georeport API allows the government, as well as third party developers, to design and develop applications that can be integrated with the previous technology and systems at the 311 call centers, so that any city that has the Open311 system up and running will be able to develop their own mobile application using the GeoReport V2 format.

Procedure

Some of the required information that is crucial to process service requests includes the latitude and longitude. Latitude and longitude will help the servers locate the exact location which is faced with a non-emergency situation such as an open pothole. The user must also register the correct and most specific address of the area. This must include information such as the street name or number, district or jurisdiction, the name of the city and added information, such as the postal code, can also be provided.

The person submitting the request must also provide his email ID; this information comes in handy if there lies some sort of ambiguity in the service request and also to update the user on the progress of his service request. The account ID must also be submitted and once the account id is submitted, information such as the full name, mobile phone number and other such details will be automatically forwarded to the Open311 system. A detailed description of the non-emergency situation is also required, for instance, if the user is reporting an incident of graffiti or vandalism, he/she needs to specify if the graffiti had been done on public property and the extent of the affected area.

Response system

To receive updates or responses to the service request, the user must provide his service id or the reference number that had been allocated to him/her. After processing the service request id, the user will be made aware of his/her service request. Two status options will appear in front of the user; the first option would be that it is open that indicates the service request has been reported. The second option would be closed which would indicate that the service request has been catered for and has been resolved.

In addition to just the status being mentioned, status notes will also be provided, which will explain why the status of the service request had been altered or why the status hasn't changed so far. The service request also would have been sorted under a service request type. In the response section, the name and specifics of the agency or local government department responsible for taking necessary action for the situation will also be listed. The service notice will include the procedure or the course of action that would be followed to address a particular service request.

The date and time of the service request are also registered to keep track of the lapsed time since the initiation of the request. The date and time of when the status was last updated is also registered. If the status of a service request is closed, then the date and time of the status update will also be mentioned. The expected date and time is also mentioned sometimes to give the users an idea of when their requests are most likely to be taken care off.

An error could also occur at the time of registering service requests. This happens when the user provides a wrong jurisdiction or postal code. This can also happen if the service requested is not one of the services listed by the Open311 system of that city or district.

The method of registering a service request is quite similar to the method of registering it with other Open311 applications. The GeoReporter mobile application is available on Android and Google Play store. After installing the application for free, the user must sign up for a GeoReporter account, after which he will be able to make 311 requests. The first step would be to choose one of the services listed in the application, such as open potholes or a broken street light. The GeoReporter offers the city performance feature as well, which enables the citizens to express concerns about their local governments' performance.

In addition, it also includes the option of Test Service where the users will get a small information package about Open311 and an internet tour of the Open311 operations. The Application also offers an app feedback option which allows users to make suggestions on what could be done to improve the application as well as what new features the users would like to see.

Geo is taken from the word geography and the reporter is what the application users are identified as, GeoReporter allows its users to report non-emergency situations and filters the service requests according to specific locations. The Georeport v2 application allows cities and technology developers to develop the application for a particular city or locality. The response system of the GeoReporter is much more advanced than any other mobile application, it even provides you with Nitti gritty details such as the date and time of the requests, and so users can get all kinds of information concerning their service requests.

Fix311 makes it easier for every city to get aboard the Open311 API train and develop open standard applications, like Fix 311 themselves. This saves enormous costs for the governments and allows them to use their funds more efficiently elsewhere. Fix 311, initially, has been just an alert applications for potholes developed by Minh Tran in 2012, after the huge snowstorm in 2010 in Washington DC. This application can basically be used from any location or any city without the user going through the hassle of downloading a range of 311 applications. It also has a service list that can be customized by the user and that constantly updates itself, while also providing the user with a list of all the service types available in an area, depending on the location of the user.

In addition to providing users with a list of services, the application is also apt at providing access to mobile website content, making Fix 311 a service request application and a mobile website that is easily accessible. It also provides users with the nifty function of being able to filter service requests according to the cities and even precincts within a particular city. Fix 311 manages this function due to its geo-boundaries detection abilities. Furthermore, it can also post links to websites and news feeds, along with making phone calls for those services that should not be or cannot be reported through an online forum, mainly because some service request types need prompt action.

Fix 311 can also filter reports for different roads that are not supported by a particular city. This application is also easy to use for the governing body because it allows them to easily update the news feed or service lists, without having to go through the hassle of downloading another new application. Furthermore, citizens can track the progress of their submitted service requests and can also cancel their requests if they wish to do so. The application is also compliant with the Open311 API and efficiently contains web-based CRM systems that manage reported cases. Lastly, the application is functional not only nationwide, but also internationally, for the low cost and pricing plans of $600 per year for small cities.

PublicStuff

PublicStuff is a convenient application that uses the Open311 API and allows the residents of a city to report minor community problems they see around them to their governments. It brings the resident one step closer to the government that they elected through a democratic process, by providing them with a convenient platform to interact with one another. The application aims to transform and promote the governing body as one of the most efficient customer service organizations, where the residents are its customers and the government's success is determined by how happy the citizens of its district are. PublicStuff brings civic service activities to the fingertips of the residents of a city, allowing unprecedented levels of civic engagement.

However, every government or organization is different and has diverse needs. PublicStuff gives the organizations or governing bodies that make use of the application the ability to completely customize the application according to their specific requirements and needs. Any government can easily brand and personalize the application and customize it to provide information and updates that are specifically relevant to their own citizens and municipalities. PublicStuff also has an extremely useful feature called 'MiniApps' which makes a wide range of information available to its users on topics such as city events, trash collection schedules, transit information and the location of animal adoption centers. It also allows its primary users to select the service request type according to the most prevalent community issues in their areas. Furthermore, it provides users a range of options to connect to its services, as it is available on numerous platforms like Apple, Android, and Windows 8 and Blackberry operating servers. In addition, PublicStuff can be utilized via a text message and it provides users with a toll-free number on which they can call and report the issues they want to see addressed.

This application allows users to connect with various other social platforms like social networking sites by enabling them to share their reported service requests on Twitter or Facebook. This feature helps increase the accountability of the staff responsible for addressing the service requests and enhances the transparency of the process by keeping it out in the open for everyone to monitor the progress being made on a particular service request. In order to make this application more accessible to as many types of communities as possible, it has the nimble feature of 'Instant Translation'.

The Instant Translation feature can translate a service request that is made in any language to the language of the user's choosing. For example, if an English-speaking organization receives a service request from a user in French, the application will translate it into English for understanding and then translate the organization's reply back into French for the user's benefit. PublicStuff also strengthens the relationship between a community and their governing body by enabling the governing body to constantly update their residents on the status of their service requests. It does so by sending its users Push Notifications about the stage their service request has reached. The Push Notifications can also be used for sending out emergency alerts.

PublicStuff improves the efficiency of the internal staff of an organization through a number of extremely helpful features. The application automatically assigns incoming service requests to the concerned member of an organization's staff, leading to a smooth flow of the whole process and ultimately increasing the efficiency of the organization. The application also allows organizations to assign specific individual tasks to people, along with delegating different workflow steps, thus increasing the efficiency of the functions performed. The tools provided by this application enable organizations to visualize the service request on a map, due to support features like its ESRI integration with Geographic Information System (GIS) mapping.

At a glance, the employees of an organization can easily pinpoint the various areas that are prone to different types of issues specific to a city, organization or institution and take preemptive measures to ensure that the same kind of community issue does not repeatedly arise. Overall, the creators of PublicStuff strive to make their application extremely compatible with any of the various enterprise solutions that an organization or government makes use of, while also providing customized reporting tools that enable organizations to make sound decisions based on the most precise and relevant data on hand. For example, it has useful reporting features that inform its host organization and users about statistics regarding user engagement levels along with average staff response times.

PublicStuff is used by over 200 organizations and cities around America. One of the prominent users of PublicStuff is the city of New York. Although the residents of New York can still make use of the city's traditional 311 system, which is accessible through a website and application as well, the conventional 311 system does not allow users to keep track of their service requests. PublicStuff resolves that issue by providing users with a speedy way of reporting their community concerns, along with pictures and location-based coordinates. It also guarantees accountability, as it constantly updates the user about various facts regarding whether or not a service request has been received by a particular department, along with providing them with information about how and when the issue they reported is being resolved. PublicStuff sounds like the ideal method of reporting and keeping track of community issues, but unfortunately for cities like New York, which haven't officially subscribed to it, that is not how the application works.

In cities where the application only exists as a third-party platform, the city officials and governments have no incentive to respond and neither are they obliged to. The negligence that this allows is apparent from PublicStuff's New York page, which is overflowing with service requests and reports regarding various community issues that have either not yet been acknowledged by the city officials or, if they have been acknowledged, they are yet to be addressed by the concerned authorities. Furthermore, it frequently happens that often when the city officials claim to have addressed and fixed a problem, the application does not indicate the progress made on the service request. Citizens have to find out the progress made on their community requests through other mediums, such as news reports, which inform the public when an issue has been resolved.

This is an important issue that the developers of PublicStuff openly acknowledge. The developers of this application refer to the requests made to cities that have not yet subscribed to its services as 'orphan requests' and they admit to the ineffectiveness of such use of the application. In contrast, a city like Philadelphia that has subscribed to the application, reports having submitted over 12,000 service requests out of which about 90 percent have been completed and are reported by the application as addressed along with details regarding the process.

Nevertheless, PublicStuff is not completely useless even in cities that have yet to subscribe to its services. PublicStuff still performs the function of providing a simplified tool for encouraging civic involvement and forming harmonious and helpful communities out of citizens that own smartphones. Even if it does nothing else, PublicStuff helps citizens understand their government better and informs them of various ways in which they can help improve the workings of their government. Applications like PublicStuff serve as a constant reminder to the residents of a city that the welfare of their community is also their responsibility.

PublicStuff, the New York based system that enables citizens to making service requests to their government in real-time, has recently been reported to be able to raise around five million dollars in additional funding for further research and development. The firm's representative informed the general public that the main financiers were two organizations called The Knight Foundation and FirstMark Capital, in addition to its existing investors. The new funds are basically going to be utilized for the expansion of the PublicStuff team and the reach of the services provided by the PublicStuff application to a growing number of countries all around the world. The PublicStuff platform can not only be utilized by different governments, but it can also be used by educational institutes and landlords who rent out residencies. Overall, it can be used by any person or organization that has to frequently manage service requests on a daily basis.

Furthermore, even though the PublicStuff application does not provide citizens a link to the highest government officials at the federal level, officials on a more local level can easily be accessed through this application, effectively addressing small-scale problems in a timely manner. PublicStuff has proven itself to be so effective that it was even featured in Forbes magazine as one of America's most promising companies. Recently, the PublicStuff application also launched in Philadelphia as Philly311 and was an immensely helpful tool in mitigating the effects of Hurricane Sansdy, with over three thousand service requests submitted from citizens to the city staff. The citizens of Philadelphia were constantly informed about the progress of the work and damage reports.

Regardless of its success, the application's business model could not avoid facing any challenges in terms of funding. But the developer of PublicStuff, Lily Liu, said that at the prospects of the enormous cost savings guaranteed by the implementation of PublicStuff, it wasn't entirely difficult to convince the governments to invest, with a guaranteed return on that investment in terms of saved costs in less than six months. The organization behind PublicStuff also has dedicated team members who help public officials in the transition of moving from traditional 311 contact centers to a more advanced platform of PublicStuff. With the use of this system, cities have experienced a surge in activism and community groups such as environmentalists. The organization responsible for PublicStuff is continuously working on improving the functions of this application, while also adding to its tools.

CHAPTER 8

Open311 Open Source Projects

The open311 utilizes a number of apps to establish a communication channel between the government officials and the citizens. This section will help you understand the open311 open source projects that play a significant role in helping public service departments improve their services. After reading this section, you would be able to understand the difference between different open source projects and other open311 software or applications. The section looks at enterprise solutions, open311 client libraries, open source projects and open source apps, integrated open311 apps and issue reporting apps. So, let's begin.

Overview of Open311 Open Source Projects

There are a number of open source projects that have either been developed around the Open311 specification and protocol or can be developed to work with the open standard specification. The most well-known open source projects are the two versions of GeoReporter. The GeoReport API permits different developers to create applications that can both view and report community issues to the responsible governments. These interactions are termed as 'service requests' and have previously been conventionally handled by either phone-based contact centers or custom, online web forums deployed by the governing body of a city.

The GeoReport API makes it easier for both third party developers and governments to collaborate and develop new technologies and applications that can efficiently and conveniently integrate with the existing official contact centers established for the purpose of addressing civic issues. The current versions of GeoReporter are focused on reporting service requests for location based, non-emergency community issues like broken street lights, aggressive animals, potholes, etc.

The GeoReport version 2 has server software that is server applications that provide an API endpoint and are able to manage and receive reports regarding civic issues. Examples of server software which make use of GeoReporter are FixMyStreet and Mark-a-Spot. There are also many client applications that are open source projects, Client applications are software that interacts with the Open311 server by connecting to an application programming interface (API), for example Open311 Facebook and the GeoReport Open311 Android and Apple applications.

Various dashboards can also be developed using the Open311 API. A well-known example of a dashboard which was designed using the Open311 API is The

Daily Brief, which constantly provides users with updates regarding events and issues of their choosing. Client libraries are also Open311 open source projects. Client libraries basically make it easier to develop client applications that work with the Open311 specification. The majority of the client libraries has been developed by the technology-oriented nonprofit organization named Code for America. Furthermore, there are also many different test suites that are available, which assist applications in verifying whether their server is compliant with the Open311 specification.

We have discussed various third party apps and other API integrated applications that help government and citizens work together towards the betterment of their cities. Let's discuss the various open311 open source projects and software to have a look at the complete picture. Below, we will discuss various apps and software utilized by the 3-1-1 call centers individually to eliminate any confusion that you might have.

Open311 Issue Reporting Apps

There are various open311 issue reporting apps that allow citizens to report a non-emergency issue easily through their smart phone and other hand-held devices. The major global open311 issue reporting apps include Kajoo, FillthatHole, HeyGov!, FixCity, Mark a Spot, Fix 311 (iPhone and Android), PublicStuff, FixMyStreet.CA, Love Clean Streets, FixMyStreet (used in the UK), FixMyStreet NZ, FixMyStreet.KR, FiksGataMi, GeoReporter, Ushahidi, GeoTrac, Buiten Beter (used in Netherlands), Neat Streets, Niet Ok (used in Netherlands), Indre By Lokaludvalg (used in Denmark),

CitySourced, How's My Street, Otro Bache (used in Spain), Citizen FYI, EveryMap (used in Australia) and Kiirti (used in India).

City Integrated open311 Apps

The most commonly used city integrated open311 apps include Fix It Plano, DC 311 Facebook, Citizen Connect iPhone App, 311 Pix iPhone App, iBurgh iPhone App, Citizen Reports iPhone, Tell Me@1823 (Hong Kong) and 311Direct . Among the above-mentioned apps, only Fix It Plano is powered by the PublicStuff application. The multi-city integrated apps include GeoReporter, PublicStuff, SeeClickFix, Connect, CitySourced iPhone app, Government Outreach iPhone app, GovQA, Maerker Brandenburg (used in Germany) and CivicPlus Citizen Request Tracker iPhone app.

Open311 open source projects

The open311 open source projects include GeoReporter, FixMyStreet (iPhone & Android), Ushahidi iPhone app, Ushahidi Android app, Ushahidi WinMobile app, Ushahidi j2me, Oil Reporter app, Social DC app and Portland Citizen Reports.

Open311 service Software

The most commonly used open311 service software services include SeeClickFix, CitySourced, PublicStuff, GORequest, GovQA, Agent511, CitiVox and CrowdMap. The service software allows citizens to report complaints and request information through their handheld devices.

Client Libraries for open311 Apps

The client libraries include various programming languages that develop specific apps for various organizations. For the development of open311 apps, developers form The Code for America and various other technology-based firms use a specific set of client libraries. The client libraries for open311 apps include PHP, Ruby Gem, Java, Node.js, C#, Python and Clojure.

311 Enterprise Solutions

The enterprise solution systems provide strong web-based, integrated case management systems that allow 3-1-1 representatives to handle citizen complaints and requests in an orderly manner. The most commonly used enterprise solutions include Lagan311, Oracle-Siebel, Motorola, Microsoft CRM, GovQA, Government Outreach, ActiveGovernment, AINS System 311, Publisafe, QScend Technologies Inc. and IntelliGov.

Most of these systems allow 3-1-1 call centers to handle non-emergency incidents by using the web-based tools that make the operations easy and hassle-free. The most well-known enterprise solution type is CRM or citizen relationship management tool that contains an incredibly comprehensive database that helps 3-1-1 agents to proactively handle non-emergency situations.

We hope by now you have a clear understanding of different open311 apps and software that are used by both citizens and the public officials to improve the cities. To help you understand things better, we will discuss the use of CRM in the implementation of Minneapolis 3-1-1 call center in the next section. We will discuss the implementation of 3-1-1 call center through a case study.

CASE STUDY

This section of the book will discuss a case study regarding building a 3-1-1 open system in the city of Minneapolis. The section will highlight the goals, objectives and implementation of the 3-1-1 call center in the city of Minneapolis. It will also include everything from the 3-1-1 call center planning to the implementation of the goals and objectives. In addition, the section will discuss the budget, marketing and education, results management, CRM software and a Minneapolis non-emergency services audit. The section will also highlight the effect of 3-1-1 system for the homeland security and 9-1-1.

Building 3-1-1 Minneapolis Call Center

Overview

In 1996, the city officials decided to improve the city's public service through the implementation of the 3-1-1 call center. Research was conducted in the city of Minneapolis to determine the possibilities for a service like open 3-1-1. According to the study, more than 16,000 calls were placed in the city, among which dozens were dropped or cancelled and sent to voicemails without a response. The research also found that many citizens had a hard time locating an operator. Most of the time, the citizens were unable to find the right information through general inquiry departments. In addition, the study stated that most citizens dropped the calls before they could receive the required information due to long waiting time.

The public inquiry departments used a number of systems to track and act upon a citizen's request, including sticky notes and Microsoft office applications; however, the call center databases were not sophisticated or efficient in operation. The city recognized the need for better coordination among the different public departments that are involved with general public service. In order to develop an efficient public service system for the improved cross-functional services, the city applied for a grant from the Department of Justice Office of Community Oriented Policing Services or COPS. In 2003, the grant was approved and the city received enough funding to develop an improved public service center known as the Minneapolis 3-1-1 centers. The grant was used along with other funds from the different city departments to create the city's first 3-1-1 call center and customer relationship management center.

The inauguration of the Minneapolis call center was in early 2006, with more than 96 services for which citizens could request help or inquiry. The center has a complete staff with trained customer service agents, team leaders, managers, analysts and supervisors. The evidence provided by the history of calls received proved that the first few years were excessively successful and well-received by the citizens of the city of Minneapolis. The majority of the calls was placed by the citizens regarding information about the public services and specific non-emergency services.

Today, the 3-1-1 project is providing a wide variety of public services to the citizens. The city officials, the management and the staff of the 3-1-1 project is constantly looking for ways to improve the service.

The Evolution of 3-1-1 Non-Emergency Services

Before the inception of 3-1-1 services, 9-1-1 was the sole public service platform that handled all the emergency and non-emergency calls placed by the U.S. citizens. The non-emergency calls included citizens' inquiries regarding office addresses, minor neighborhood complaints, domestic problems and other inquiries that were not actual emergencies. This led to great confusion and sometimes, actual emergency calls were dropped due to the large volume of non-emergency calls on the line. The 3-1-1 non-emergency services were developed to separate the emergency and non-emergency public departments so that the public can have hassle-free access to the city management, and the management can have a hassle-free operation.

The Baltimore police department implemented a 3-1-1 non-emergency services department in 1996. Today, the department handles most of the city's non-emergency services. The Federal Communications Commission started using 3-1-1 as a non-emergency service number in the year 1997. Similarly, various cities adopted 3-1-1 as their non-emergency service number throughout the United States. According to a research study, in 2008, nearly 50 cities in the United States adopted 3-1-1 as the non-emergency number for non-emergency inquiries and other non-emergency services.

Minneapolis 3-1-1Call Center

The vision of the Minneapolis 3-1-1 call center: *"With one call, Minneapolis citizens get around-the-clock, customer-friendly access to City services and information. The City provides a timely response, efficient service delivery and continuous improvement of services based on an improved ability to measure and track performance."*

The main purpose of the Minneapolis 3-1-1 call center was to provide general public services to the more than 400,000 citizens of the Minneapolis city. The aim was to provide quick access to the city's municipal services, information and other non-emergency services information, including the non-emergency police services.

3-1-1 and CRM

The Minneapolis 3-1-1 Call Center combined both the city-operated model and the police-operated model. The 3-1-1 project offers the citizens a complete solution for everyday business operations and other non-emergency situations, to help citizens reduce costs and minimize overall risks associated with non-emergency services. The Minneapolis 3-1-1 project uses CRM software developed by Lagan Technologies to enable Minneapolis management to effectively coordinate public operations through more efficient and responsive departments; the CRM software allows the management to create an effective data base for the all the public services for effective operations. The previous applications and software used by the public service departments were not as effective and were usually hard to control as compared to the new CRM system. The CRM system allows public service departments to have a consistent follow-up on various citizen inquiries. The efficient database allows management and various departments to coordinate and respond to non-emergency situations quickly.

According to Minneapolis Mayor R.T. Rybak *"Our new 3-1-1 system has so many benefits, not just for the city departments, but especially for the residents, who now have a simple, streamlined way to access city information and services."*

According to a survey result, 65 percent of the calls placed to 9-1-1 are actually non-emergency calls. The biggest advantage of the 3-1-1 system is that it will keep the 9-1-1 service open for serious emergency calls that need a quick response. The 3-1-1 system handles inquiries about the city services and non-emergency situations that include small-scale thefts, threatening calls, suspicious activity and domestic intrusion. The city's coordinator's office supervises both the 9-1-1 and 3-1-1 coordinated operations.

Creation of Results Minneapolis

The implementation of the 3-1-1 call center brought many changes in the various departments of the city including police and results-based public management. The 3-1-1 call center was developed to perform multipurpose tasks that would contribute towards an improved city environment through coordination among the different departments. Today, the 3-1-1 call center provides citizens with a reliable 24/7 service that offers quick response and action through staff agents and CRM system.

The Results Minneapolis was created to improve the leadership efficiency through feedback and response from the citizens contained in the CRM system. The system utilizes CRM software designed by Logan technologies, which allows various departments to coordinate and provide a better response time for specific requests.

The Need for 3-1-1in Minneapolis

Before the establishment of the Minneapolis 3-1-1 call center, the city officials conducted thorough research regarding the non-emergency services in the city and found out that there is a lack of focus and consistency in citizen request handling. The inconsistency of the system was creating a stream of unsatisfied requests. In addition, most of non-emergency calls were being placed to the 9-1-1 call center.

Minneapolis Non-emergency Services Audit

Before the emergence of the 3-1-1 call center, the city officials hired a well-known consulting firm, McKinsey and Company to conduct in-depth research regarding the city's emergency and non-emergency service and other public services. The results of the research showed that the public service departments failed to coordinate well to provide better services to the citizens. Most of the calls placed by citizens to the public service departments were not answered or went to voicemail.

In addition, the research showed that the departments failed to maintain consistency of operations within the departments, which led to overall inefficiency of the system. The report suggested that the city should create a balance between different public service departments through a centralized center that would not only improve public service, but also make it easy for the officials to manage the various public service departments. Therefore, the Minneapolis 3-1-1 center plan was born. The report suggested city officials use a centralized approach to manage public service through CRM and the 3-1-1 call center.

The results of the report suggested city officials:

- Create an open 3-1-1 call center
- Develop a software system to keep track of all the calls
- Upgrade the telephone systems or install new systems to accommodate the large call volume to the 3-1-1 service.

- Establish 3-1-1 system as a backup for the 9-1-1 call center.

According to the McKinsey results, all public organizations of Minneapolis should be involved in the implementation of the centralized service. The report suggested that the city officials should create a shared service for all the public departments so they coordinate better regarding the public services.

Call Coordination and Management

The research identified call coordination and call management as the most important aspects of the overall project. A caller might place a serious emergency call to 3-1-1, and a caller might place a non-emergency call to 9-1-1. This is why it is very important for the CSA or staff members to recognize the nature of the call and then transfer it to the right center.

For example, if a 3-1-1 center receives an emergency call regarding a residential fire, a 3-1-1 agent should forward the call to the 9-1-1 center. The 3-1-1 call center agent should not hang up until he is certain that the call has been received by the 9-1-1 center. Similarly, if the 9-1-1 call center receives a non-emergency call, it should immediately transfer it to the 3-1-1 call center.

After the research, the city officials realized that the problems faced by the public service departments can only be met through a 3-1-1 call center. The aim of creating a 3-1-1 call center was to:

- Reduce the volume of abandoned calls and misrouted calls
- Reduce the large volume of listed numbers in the blue-page directory
- Reduce the burden of calls placed to the 9-1-1 call center
- Offer timely assistance to the citizens
- Consolidated various call centers to create a centralized center
- Enhance tracking system to analyze citizen needs

These goals and their implementation are discussed in detail in the next section.

Departments Rolled into the 3-1-1 Center

The report advised city officials to create a centralized public center by merging or consolidating different public centers. For this purpose, the city officials rolled various departments into the 3-1-1 center in order to achieve a centralized public department. In addition, large amounts of phone numbers were erased from the telephone book. The city officials have rolled various departments into the 3-1-1 call center including animal control, police administration, graffiti hotline, police e-reports, city hall operators, impound lot, community planning, economic development, police precincts, city clerk, budget office, regulatory services, environmental health, TTY/TDD numbers, Minneapolis emergency communications center (MECC) activities and housing inspections.

The Minneapolis 3-1-1 call center consists of nearly 26 highly trained CSAs, or customer representative agents, who handle customer queries and requests from 7 a.m. to 11 p.m., Monday through Friday. Voice messages are recorded in the system and the agents respond to the messages on the next working day. In addition, the citizens can use the self-service option and the call center's website for specific information or inquiries. All the inquiries received by the CSAs are transferred to specific departments immediately after the request is made.

Development of Knowledge Base

As mentioned above, the 3-1-1 center opened various opportunities for the public sector. One such opportunity was the development of the knowledge base. A detailed knowledge base was developed as a part of the Minneapolis 3-1-1 project. The knowledge base uses the Lagan Knowledge Tool to provide relevant information to the citizens.

According to a research study, nearly fifty percent of the calls placed in the 3-1-1 call center is mainly about information related to non-emergency events including small-scale thefts and public safety. The statistics of a research report show that almost twenty-two percent of the calls placed in the 3-1-1 call center is related to public safety. Twelve percent of the calls are about permits and licenses, and about eleven percent regarding recycling and garbage. The other knowledge base categories include animal control, commercial property disputes, parking services, housing and other non-emergency services.

Interfaces with the 3-1-1 System

After the development of the 3-1-1 project, the city officials created a clear interface between the CRM application and the public service departments, such as a housing Inspections application (an application that tracks housing complaints), sidewalk database (that keeps track of snow and ice complaints), animal control application (that handles complaints regarding animals, mostly stray dogs). The 3-1-1 center representatives have direct access to the police E report systems, computer aided towing systems and the city website. In addition, the government officials have added Regulatory Services' KIVA system to give 3-1-1 representatives a better and easy access to data.

Budget for the 3-1-1 call Center

According to the city report, the 3-1-1 call center utilizes around $2.6 million annually. All of the city departments fund the 3-1-1 project, according to the proportion of work performed by the 3-1-1 service for a specific center. The software cost for the 3-1-1 project was around $3.2 million. The other costs include facility costs (around $1.2 million) professional services costs (around $1.8 million) computer workstations costs (around $74,000) and CRM license cost ($175,000).

The 3-1-1 Build-out

The Minneapolis 3-1-1 call center is built inside the Third Precinct building's third floor. The total area occupied by the call center is about 5,500 square feet. The offices located inside the call center are incorporated into the Procenter and Automatic Call Distribution (ACD) software. The call center provides its agents with up-to-date technology, including flat-screen Dell computers that allow 3-1-1 representatives to have a multifunctional system for greater productivity and efficiency. The call center has a continual power supply with generator backup systems that ensure that the systems keep running even in case of emergency.

In case of emergency, the 9-1-1 agents can relocate to the 3-1-1 call center to perform operations. Half of the workstations in the 3-1-1 call center is configured to work as 9-1-1 operator stations and the rest of the workstations are configured to work as 9-1-1 dispatch stations.

Marketing of the 3-1-1 Minneapolis Call Center

The marketing campaign for the 3-1-1 call center began weeks before its launch in early 2006. The citizens were informed about the 3-1-1 call center through various advertisements and campaigns that focused on the importance of 3-1-1 center and its services. The marketing and education still continues. Even after years, citizens are still reminded about how to place a call to 3-1-1 center through public seminars and campaigns so that everyone knows how to reach a public official in case of a non-emergency situation.

The education eliminated the large number of call non-emergency calls that were accidentally placed to the 9-1-1 center. The department of public service still educates people to make sure that citizens understand the right use of both 9-1-1 and 3-1-1 services.

Effect of 3-1-1 Call Center on 9-1-1

Before the launch of 3-1-1 call center, all emergency and non-emergency related calls were placed to the 9-1-1 center. This increased the load of calls on the 9-1-1 service and sometimes the emergency related calls could not get through because of the large volume of calls placed in the centers. After the launch of 3-1-1 call center, the 9-1-1 call center was totally dedicated to the emergency related calls. With coordination, both call centers handle the non-emergency and emergency related calls. For example, if an emergency related call is accidentally placed i the 3-1-1 call center, the 3-1-1 agents forward the call to the 9-1-1 centers and vice versa.

The steady coordination among the centers ensures smooth service and satisfied citizens. The operations of both the centers are closely monitored. The assistant city coordinator is responsible for monitoring both 9-1-1 and 3-1-1 services. The assistant coordinator reports to the city coordinator.

Effect of 3-1-1 Call Center on Homeland Security

The 3-1-1 system is consolidated with various government and regulatory systems. The purpose of merging different public service departments with the 3-1-1 system was to create a centralized unit to serve the city better. The 3-1-1 call center plays an important role in homeland security. The officials of the city of

Minneapolis have incorporated the 3-1-1 project in the homeland security and crisis management plan. This has allowed the city officials to manage both man-made and natural disasters through the help of the 3-1-1 call center.

In addition, the 3-1-1 system is implemented with the Minneapolis Business Continuity Plan, which is based on the National Incident Management System. The plan includes the steps that should be taken in case of an emergency. The plan identifies the 3-1-1 call center as a crucial part of the system, as it develops a strong communication link between the regulatory services and the public.

3-1-1 in Action

After the launch of the 3-1-1 service, the city of Minneapolis faced severe damage that resulted from the collapse of the I-35W Bridge in early 2007. The 3-1-1 services received hundreds of non-emergency calls, including general information regarding the bridge collapse, information regarding road closure, information regarding alternate route, charity information, Red Cross information and information regarding public viewing. The 3-1-1 center also received calls to request tracking, which included media requests, information regarding reporting and tracking services, personal property and vehicle information, eyewitness reports, victim and missing person information and donated services information, as well as traffic control complaints. This proved that the 3-1-1 system is capable of crisis management.

Effect of 3-1-1 Call Center on Minneapolis Police Department

The 3-1-1 call center has a significant impact on the Minneapolis police department. The service requests for the Minneapolis police department include National Night-Out, canine appearance request, E-Reports, Suspicious activity reports, homicide tips, parking complaints, complaints regarding police officers, ride-along requests, 9-1-1 transcript requests, graffiti complaint/reporting, crime statistics, seized vehicle search, crime prevention and assistance requests. The consolidation of several police departments in the city of Minneapolis has reduced the call volume for non-police or non-emergency related calls.

Major Goals of the Minneapolis 3-1-1 Call Center

The management of the city of Minneapolis uses 3-1-1 projects to provide public services to the citizens and to improve citizens' satisfaction regarding non-emergency services. The basic goals of the Minneapolis 3-1-1 Call Center include:

- Building an effective communication system on which citizens can rely.
- Developing a healthy infrastructure to ensure the safety of the city and its inhabitants.
- Providing a quality non-emergency services to the citizens.
- Creating an effective environment that contributes towards the economic development and overall cost reduction.

Completed Deliverables of the Minneapolis 3-1-1 Call Center

Following are the completed deliverable of the Minneapolis 3-1-1 Call Center:

1. Enhance citizen's satisfaction through improved non-emergency services.
2. Use existing resources to develop efficiencies in different public service departments.
3. Improve the overall system of the service request and tracking.
4. Use results management to improve services provided to the citizens.
5. Use 3-1-1 services to enhance homeland security.
6. Contribute towards all public service departments, especially 9-1-1.
7. Develop policing capabilities to track suspicious situations and provide a quick solution.

Other Deliverables of the Minneapolis 3-1-1 Call Center

The other deliverables of the Minneapolis 3-1-1 project include:

- Identify the problem areas, rectify and share lessons with other communities to promote 3-1-1 services.
- Create a management information system to implement 3-1-1 project goals for better public service.
- Develop online permit services.

- Upgrade the telephone systems for a better call management.
- Introduce multilingual resources to reduce language barriers among the citizens.
- Introduce new telephone services including web chat, skills routing and call recording.
- Use personalized surveys and correspondence for better response and feedback on services.
- Support human and health service requests with quick response and action.

Goal Implementation

The Minneapolis 3-1-1 project has several goals, including implementation of 3-1-1 services, ease of access, improved homeland security and use of results management. The city officials took specific approaches to attain all the goals. This section highlights the necessary steps taken to achieve the project goals.

Goal #1: Enhance citizen's satisfaction through improved non-emergency services

The city developed a single service telephone number that is easy to remember and use. The telephone lines are open 24 hours a day, staffed 16 hours every day, excluding the weekends. For the non-staffed hours, public can access the service by voicemail. The telephone, mail and web requests are handled by a central body of the 3-1-1 system. The consolidated system is used for the email requests and general inquiries.

Most of the calls received by the 3-1-1 center is regarded city information and are handled by the CSA or customer service agents who are well trained in the field. Additional telephone lines are open to citizens who do not speak English as their first language. CSA agents provide tracking numbers to all the callers so they can easily learn about the progress of their request. CSA agents provide timely response with appropriate action to all citizen requests.

Goal # 2: Use existing resources to develop efficiencies

For the project to be successful, it is crucial that the 3-1-1 service has an efficient system in place. The CRM software provides a real-time information database that contains the names, tracking numbers and addresses of all the callers. In addition to the CRM, a central call system was put in place and various other call units were consolidated to create one effective system for quick response.

Goal # 3: Improve the overall system of service request and tracking

According to a survey, this goal has been served very well. All the calls made to the 3-1-1 service center is regularly tracked and routed to designated specialized agents electronically through the CRM software. Web, telephone and email requests are treated equally and are handled by specialized agents. Everyday requests and inquiries are handled by the CSA agents through the Lagan Knowledge Base. Over a certain time period, the system generates reports that are analyzed for crime patterns that usually occur.

Goal # 4: Use results management to improve services provided to the citizens

Results-based management is a strategy that uses feedback to achieve certain strategic goals. Results Minneapolis, a results-based management system for the city, was developed in early 2006. The goal of the system is to understand the cultural change in the city leaders. 3-1-1 services provide data in the form of citizen feedback to help the results management system for an improved city.

Goal # 5: Use 3-1-1 services to enhance homeland security

The Minneapolis 3-1-1 center is also used as a backup 9-1-1 center, should the 9-1-1 call center becomes inaccessible. The city officials have implemented a plan where the 3-1-1 call center can be used as a backup center for the 9-1-1 call center in case of serious national emergencies.

Goal # 6: Contribute towards all public service departments, especially 9-1-1

As discussed earlier in the section, one of the major reasons for the creation of the 3-1-1 call center was to provide an additional service for non-emergency calls so that the 9-1-1 center can be strictly open to serious emergency situations. According to a report, the non-emergency calls placed to the 9-1-1 center was reduced by 17 percent after the launch of the 3-1-1 call center. In the year 2007, the number of non-emergency calls was reduced to 34 percent.

The 3-1-1 system records and provides responses to non-emergency domestic situations and small-scale thefts, which were previously handled by the 9-1-1 center. In addition, the 3-1-1 center also handles small-scale crimes through the Police E-Reports program.

Goal # 7: Develop policing capabilities to track suspicious situations

In recent years, the city's crime prevention department was significantly reduced due to a low budget. However, with the launch of the 3-1-1 call center, many of the crime prevention operations are handled centrally, including calls regarding suspicious activities in the city. In the recent past, the crime prevention officer handled crime prevention. Today, crime prevention is handled through CRM.

Today's system is far more efficient than the previous system, as the CRM provides substantial historical information regarding various crimes. In addition, crime reports generated through the CRM system to analyze crime patterns and help agents control crime in the city. The reports can also provide agents with a detailed analysis of emerging trends that can be prevented before they occur.

Other Goals of the 3-1-1 Center

The Minneapolis 3-1-1 center achieved various other goals that improved overall public service. Some of these goals are mentioned below:

- Developed an efficient management system for the public work. The 3-1-1 center became the front end for the community planning and economic development (CPED) center.
- The 3-1-1 center and the CPED provided citizens with a service to help them with mortgage foreclosure.
- The online permitting services were created to allow citizens to have a quick permits for certain housing and construction work. According to a research study, the regulatory service that handles online permitting services is interested in using the 3-1-1 call center for the service.
- The 3-1-1 call center management has developed specific ways to handle calls for human and health services. The CSA staff members determine the nature of the request and forward the request to the 2-1-1 staff.
- The city had a major telephone upgrade to improve the overall efficiency of the call management system. The upgrades were created in coordination with the 3-1-1 call center for better efficiency of the call management system.
- Call recording and tracking has become a major part of the 3-1-1 call center. In addition,

skill-based routing is implemented in the call center in specified situations. For example, skill-based routing was used in the snow emergency to direct the calls to specific subject matter experts.

- To remove language barriers, the 3-1-1 call center uses a separate language line, which provides translation services to citizens who have a different native language. In addition, the call center uses a TTY capability, a web service better known as TextNet, to provide superior services to the citizens who suffer from hearing loss.

Examples of Services Provided Through the 3-1-1 Call Center

The 3-1-1 call center provides various services to the citizens of Minneapolis. The section highlights the major services provided to the citizens through the 3-1-1 call center. The most common examples of the services include non-emergency crimes services, snow and ice complaints and abandoned vehicle issues

Non-emergency crimes

Before the 3-1-1 call center, the Minneapolis officials used Teleserve reports for the non-emergency crime reports, which were taken by civilian employees or community service officers and citizen messages were sometimes impossible to understand. Most commonly the messages were hard to decipher when the caller's voice was not clear, there was distortion on the line and the caller (whose native language was other than English) was unable to clearly explain the situation.

The launch of the 3-1-1 call center allowed the city officials to review the old procedures and offer improved services to citizens who suffer from non-emergency crimes. The 3-1-1 call center was integrated by the Minneapolis police department to provide enhanced public service to the citizens. With the 3-1-1 call center, citizens have the opportunity to report a crime directly to a 3-1-1 representative or use the self-help option to report any type of crime. In addition, the Minneapolis police department also offers a secure crime reporting web feature to its partners.

Abandoned Vehicle Issues

Before the launch of the 3-1-1 call center, dealing with abandoned vehicles was a tough nut to crack. With 3-1-1 center, city officials can easily review the procedures for abandoned vehicle issues and deal with them in a timely fashion. Today, the city is able to handle abandoned vehicle issues efficiently. With the consolidated centers, the information about the abandoned vehicles can be easily sent to a specific department, which was not possible before.

The reporting of an abandoned vehicle was difficult for both parties: the reporting party and the public service departments. The main reason for this difficulty was that the citizens were not educated enough about various public service departments and therefore were unable to report an abandoned vehicle to the right department. In addition, the traffic control department was receiving more than 7,000 calls regarding abandoned vehicles, which made it impossible for them to control the non-emergency vehicle situation.

Snow and Ice Issues

Before the 3-1-1 service in the city, there was no comprehensive system in the place for snow and ice complaints. Citizens reported snow and ice complaints to the various public service departments as there was no clear guideline as to where to report these complaints. With 3-1-1, citizens can easily report snow and ice complaints and get a quick response.

The complaints are added into the Frontlink and the request is immediately forwarded to the sidewalk database, which creates an identical case copy. The identical copy is cross-referenced to the Frontlink database. As the representative or the inspector assigned to the case works on the case, the identical file in the Frontlink is automatically updated, which keeps both files in synch. In most cases, the inspector issues a warning letter and if upon re-inspection the sidewalk is still not clean, the inspector or representative updates the request in the sidewalk database.

The interface then forwards the request to the street division's work order. The street division, upon receiving the request, removes the snow and updates the work order. The sidewalk division, after ensuring that the work is done, closes the case and bills the requester or the property owner who filed the complaint.

In a nutshell, citizens of Minneapolis can report any non-emergency incident to the 3-1-1 call center. Whether it is an abandoned vehicle or snow covered sidewalk, the 3-1-1 representatives will transfer the calls to the specific departments within seconds and citizens would be able to get a quick response regarding the situation.

CONCLUSION

In an ever expanding world of hundreds of countries, thousands of cities and a staggering number of communities, the provision of non-emergency civic services is a concept that is rising in importance every day. Non-emergency civic services have been defined as those situations that do not require immediate medical or safety attention, and in which there are no prominent threats to anyone's life. For example, if the resident of a community notices a pothole in a frequently used strip of road, the individual could report it to the concerned authorities, who will then get to work on fixing the pothole.

The authorities that fixed the pothole in the road would be performing a non-emergency civic service. Similarly, if a citizen starts a movement to raise awareness about the importance of educating homeless and orphaned children, that resident would also be performing a non-emergency civic service by disseminating information among the members of a community. On the other hand, emergency civic services involve the provision of services that tackle situations in which the life of one person or the lives of a thousand or more people are at stake. Earthquake relief activities, police response to a life threatening crime and other such activities are prominent examples of emergency civic services.

Of course, activities that concentrate on emergency relief services will always be of utmost significance and are usually carried out on a much larger scale as compared to non-emergency services. Community specific, non-emergency needs cannot be ignored, deeming them equally important as emergency civic services. The provision of civic services is not only the responsibility of the multitude of governments and authoritative bodies that exist in this world, but it is the duty of each and every citizen of a society. This is because it is not possible for the governing bodies of different cities to be constantly aware of every minute problem that prevails in a city, due to the sizes of cities in the current era.

In order to ensure the smooth running of a city, its residents, along with the government, need to ensure maximum and efficient participation in civic engagement and provision of civic services. Once societies are increasingly integrated and every member of the community is dedicated to civic activities, cities will run like well-oiled machines. The efficient provision of non-emergency civic services don't just improve the operations of a city, they also vastly improve the living standard of the residents of a city along with various other economic, social and cultural advantages.

As mentioned in the sections above, civic participation is restricted to cover just one particular city or community. Participation in civic services is also an important global phenomenon due to the increasing interconnected nature and interdependence of countries brought about by the advent of technology. Technology has enabled information to travel from one place to another in next to no time. For example, the internet enables a resident of an American city to effortlessly communicate with the resident of, say, Pakistan, while incurring minimum and negligible costs. The internet doesn't only serve as an information disseminating medium for a single individual, it is also used by various organizations to collaborate with firms in far-off regions. This easy access and effortless link to various entities, all around the world, increases the impact of non-emergency civic services ten-fold, while also opening up endless possibilities and opportunities.

So how can individuals actively participate in civic services? As explained in the book, the most important thing a citizen can do to effectively engage in civic services is to ensure that they are adequately educated about the various aspects of non-emergency civic services. The residents of a city can achieve this by making efforts to acquire civic learning, and becoming fully empowered and aware as to their capabilities and responsibilities. Civic learning not only garners a sense of responsibility and awareness about significant city matters in individuals, it also prepares individuals for dealing with some trivial non-emergency civic matter that they might face. It helps an individual realize they are not useless, but an important part of the society with the ability to make a difference.

As always, the advent of technology has opened ever increasing avenues of engaging and delivering non-emergency civic services. One prominent example of the benefits of technological progress and innovation is the Open311 API that has been repeatedly mentioned and explained in minute detail throughout the book. The Open311 API, along with various other collaborate platforms and third-party applications, has made participation in and the provision of civic services an almost effortless endeavor. The development of such interactive platforms would not have been possible without the increasing integration of mobile and cellular devices in developed and developing societies all over the world; if mobile devices were not widely used, the impact of open standards like the Open311 API would have been negligible.

But the innovations in technology will not just stop there. The prevalence and creation of ever-increasing cloud-based applications and platforms are just waiting to happen. Such cloud-based servers will help empower citizens and individuals in every corner of the world, automating more and more functions and operations of a municipality.

Cloud-based software and application will open civic services to avenues of global management. These applications can easily be hosted in one location, enabling the city workers and teams to maintain and exert control over them from that one location. This convenience eliminates the need to employ extra staff that specialized in technical operations as cloud-based software can be easily used by just about anyone; all the worker or employee would need is a one-time training on how to operate the platform. Cloud-based global management also allows organizations and governments interested in the provision of non-emergency civic services to monitor separate server usage and identify any problems that might be affecting the entity's overall cloud environment.

Furthermore, due to the integrated nature of cloud-based applications that are all hosted in one location, civic service related systems and software can conveniently be updated all at once. This easy method of upgrading a system, decreases the differences between the various versions of an application being used, along with reducing compatibility issues that could arise between team members working on a common project. Moreover, the cloud-based nature of applications gives their users constant access to the current and updated software without any additional costs.

An interesting fact reported by the magazine 'Digital Trends' in February 2013 was that the number of cell-phone users, minus the tablet and internet-capable device owners, is estimated to reach around 7.3 billion by the end of 2014. That is a staggering statistic and while it is intimidating, it is also good news for all developers of applications that are cloud-based. As time goes by, the importance of mobility in almost all our everyday tasks is taking increasing precedence, posing a challenge for cloud technology to keep pace with such mobile users, by continuing to come up with viable cloud-based solutions. This is a fact that has especially important implications for civic service engagement and provision, as application mobility gives end users the power to access self-service and broad network non-emergency function, on demand and at any time.

By further integrating and implementing cloud automation technology, many governments can give their residents the power to provision their very own cloud servers and applications which can be used for the improvement of civic activity. This empowers a normal citizen and gives an individual the access to immediate and effective resources that impact civic engagement. Furthermore, broad network access implies that cloud-based applications can be used on a wide range of electronic platforms like desktops, laptops, tablets and smartphones, bringing civic services and activities within the reach of every individual possible.

Most governments and organizations that work for the provision of civic services increasingly prefer using cloud-based applications because they are extremely easy to launch and bring into operation. When cloud-based applications are paired with cloud automation, they are so simple to use that even users with no technological experience and limited technological knowledge can easily operate them. This is because automation allows such inexperienced users to launch servers and applications with a move as simple as the click of a button. Lastly, cloud automation is also useful because of its ability to make use of existing technologies and infrastructure while at the same time, strengthening the migration of old systems to cloud-based platforms.

The most glaring advantage of governments and citizens utilizing cloud-based technology is that it is an extremely cost-effective solution and very affordable for just about anyone. Furthermore, the implantation of cloud-based technology does not require the purchase of any extra infrastructure or storage because cloud-based applications require no such hassle. This makes cloud-based software a more cost effective medium for providing the necessary civic services to a community without incurring and bearing intimidating amounts of changes in infrastructure and cost. Such helpful innovations in cloud- based technology may just well be the future of civic services.

In conclusion, civic services are vital to ensure the harmonious existence of communities, cities and countries and there will never be a time where the need for active civic engagement will die out. With technology augmenting the impact of civic services, the prevalence and impact of such activities will only go upwards. As citizens become increasingly more educated about their civic responsibility and their obligation to give back to a community that does so much for them, more and more portions of the population, regardless of the demographics, will become aware of the advantages of civic services, resulting in increasing participation in civic activities.

Moreover, once the governments of different cities realize that their citizens are aware of their civic rights, they will be more liable and held responsible for ensuring that adequate resources are dedicated to the provision of civic services. Governing bodies will also become increasingly aware of the importance of creating a strong bond with the residents of their city.

The provision of civic services is a responsibility that cannot be ignored by any entity and with the advancement and prevalence of technology, more and more organizations and governments will be able to fulfill their duty efficiently. Taken to a global level, civic participation and engagement will only prolong the life of our planet, which, if not taken care, will soon be exhausted of all the resources and provisions that are so important for the continued existence of human life. By encouraging cooperation by different countries towards a collective common goal, the diplomatic relationship of various countries will be strengthened.